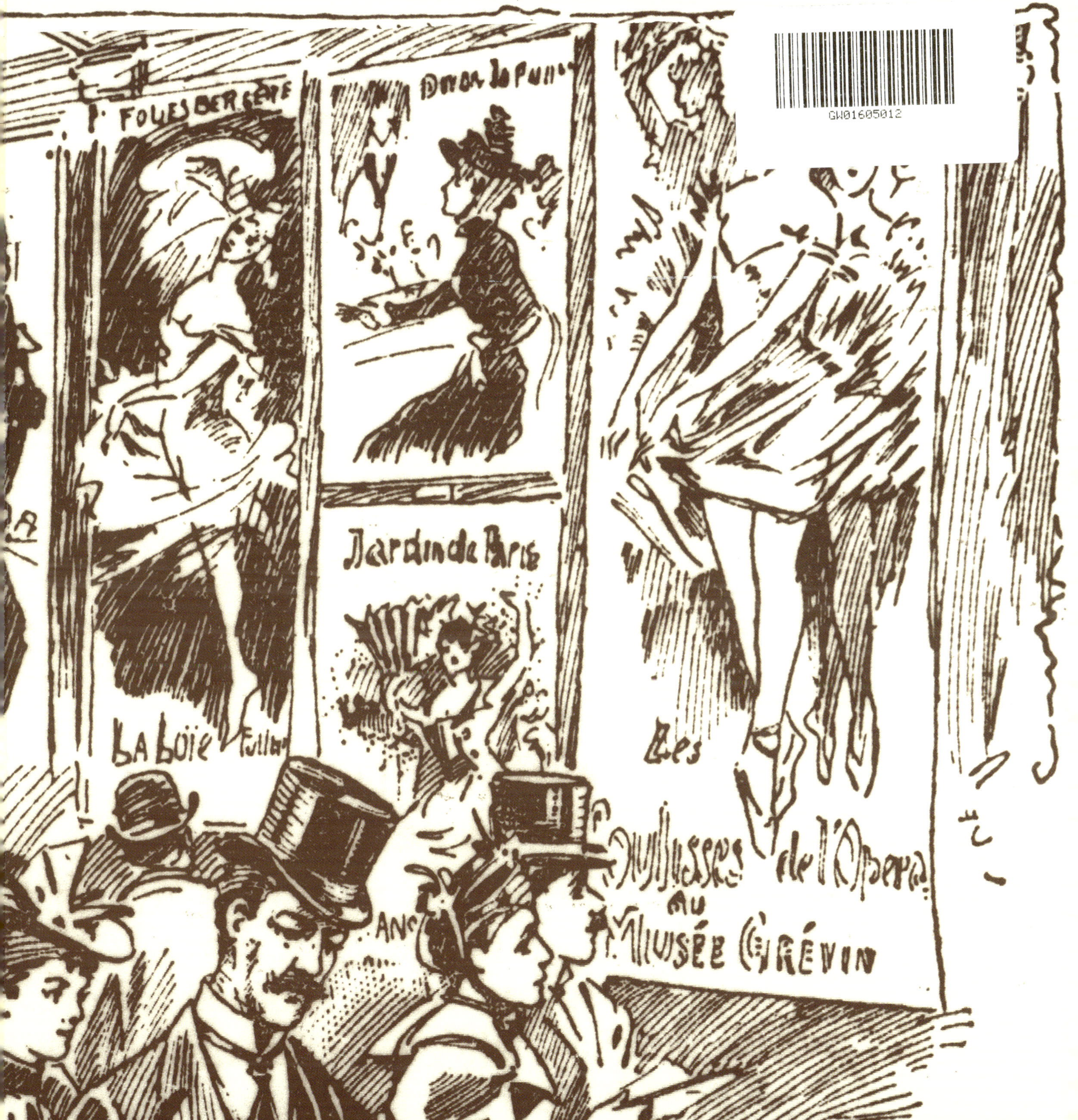
FOLIES BERGÈRE
Jardin de Paris
de l'Opera
au
Musée Grévin

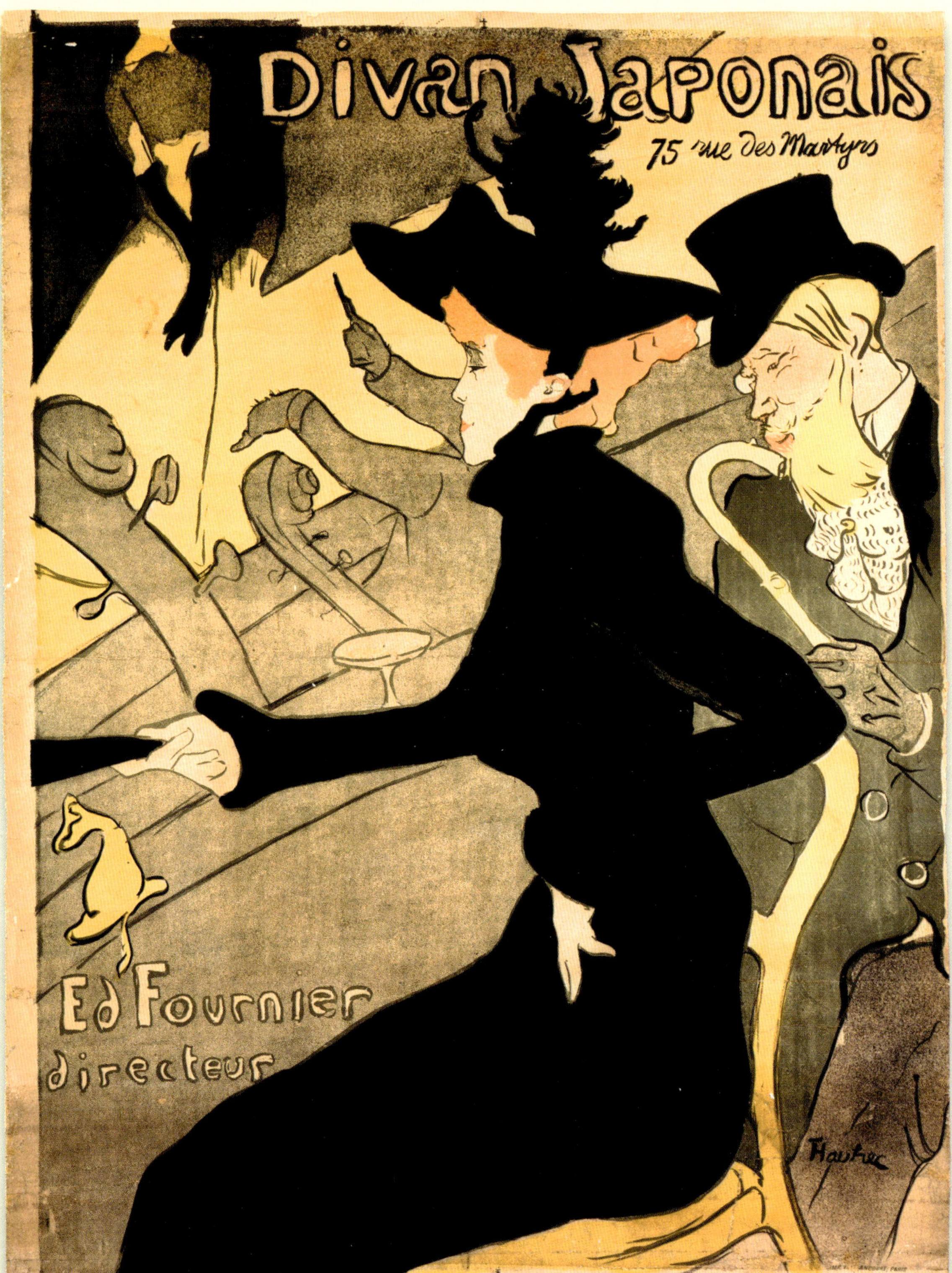
Divan Japonais
75 rue des Martyrs
Ed Fournier
directeur
HLautrec

TOULOUSE LAUTREC AND THE ART OF THE FRENCH POSTER

Howard Coutts and Claire Jones

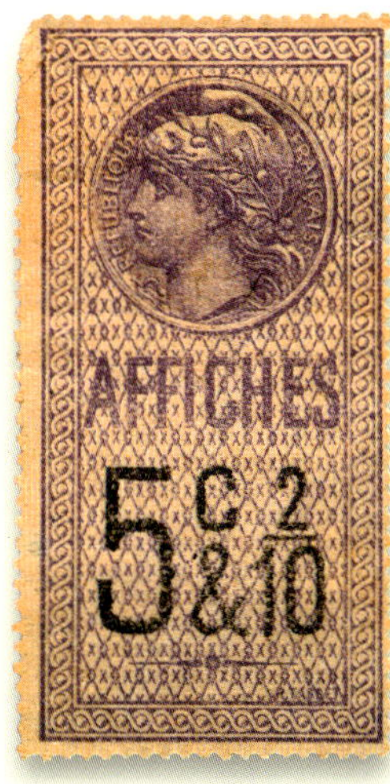

Chairman's Foreword

THE BOWES MUSEUM houses one of the great collections of French art in Britain. It was founded by John and Joséphine Bowes, who lived in Paris in the mid-nineteenth century. John Bowes had met Joséphine as an actress on the stage of the Théâtre des Variétés, a theatre that he owned and was later to provide a venue for such artists as Yvette Guilbert in the late nineteenth century. Together John and Joséphine collected over 15,000 separate objects, many from the period of the Second Empire (1852–70).

The art they collected, and the documentation they left, have provided the inspiration for a number of exhibitions we have recently devoted to French art and its antecedents in the nineteenth century. This exhibition, *Toulouse-Lautrec and the Art of the French Poster*, is concerned specifically with one theme, the art of the poster that blossomed through the work of Jules Chéret, Henri de Toulouse-Lautrec and others at the end of the nineteenth century. John Bowes, dying in 1885, would have seen the very beginnings of this, in the early work of Jules Chéret. Had he lived another ten years longer he could have enjoyed a selection of the finest and most advanced work that was shown in a special exhibition in London in 1894, at a venue called the 'Royal Aquarium'. It is a great privilege to be able to bring together a number of the exhibits, some still bearing their original exhibition number, through the courtesy of an exceptional loan from the Victoria and Albert Museum, London.

John Eccles

Chairman

Plate 1 (Inside covers)
View of the gallery of the Royal Aquarium, with posters by Chéret, Toulouse-Lautrec, Métivet and Steinlen
Illustration from The Penny Illustrated Paper, 10 Nov 1894
The British Library

Plate 2 (page 4)
Henri de Toulouse-Lautrec (1864–1901)
Divan Japonais
1894
COLOUR LITHOGRAPH
83.5 x 63.5 CM
V&A Images/Victoria & Albert Museum
An example was shown at the London poster exhibition 1894–5, No. 123 [3/6 or 17.5p]

Plate 3 (page 5)
Poster Tax Stamp
FRENCH, EARLY 20TH CENTURY, 5 x 2.5 CM
Private collection

Plate 4 (detail, opposite)
Henri de Toulouse-Lautrec (1864–1901)
Caudieux
1893
COLOUR LITHOGRAPH, 124.5 x 89 CM
Bridgeman Art Library/Private Collection
An example was shown at the London poster exhibition 1894–5, No. 125 [8/- or 40p]

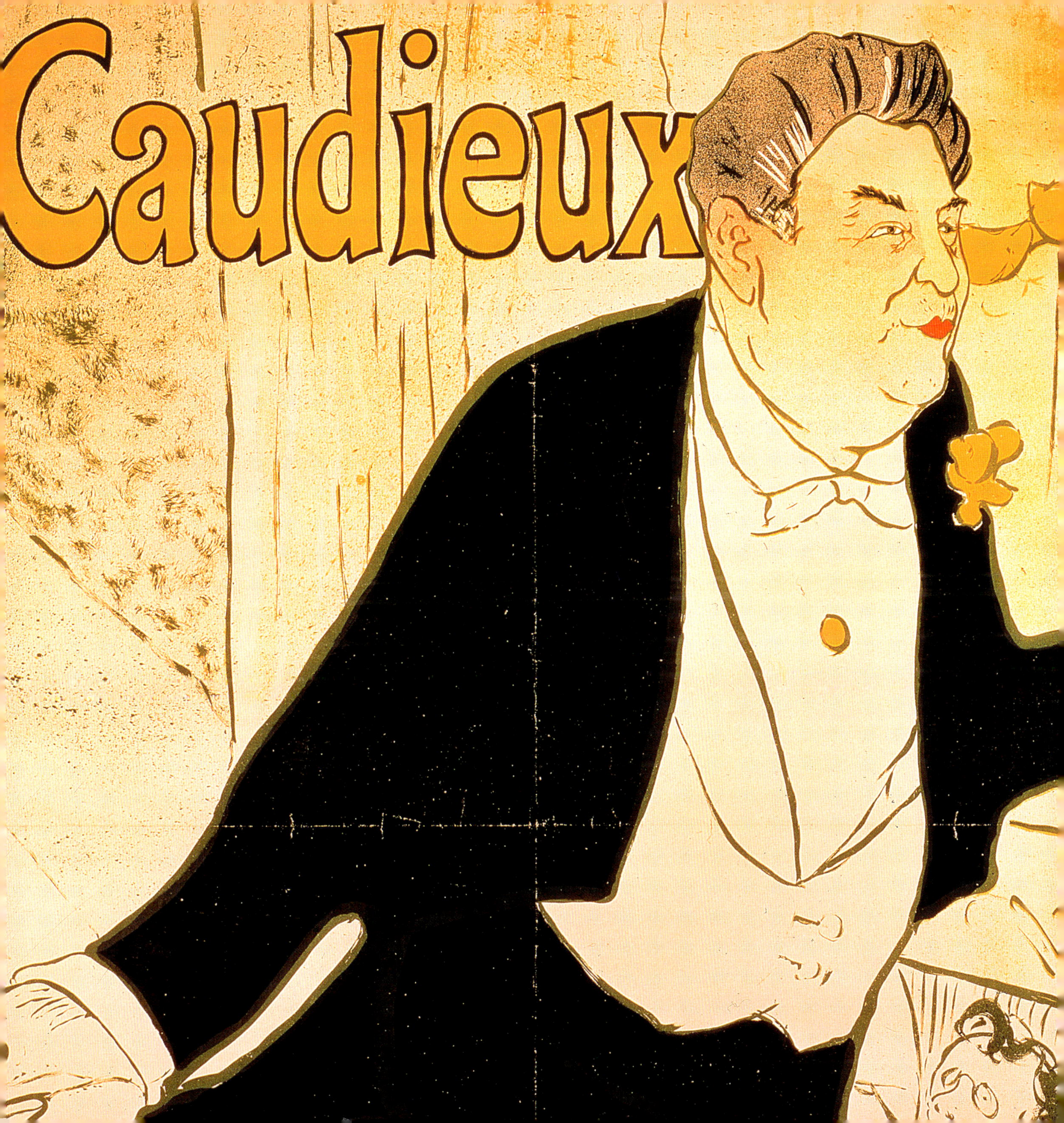
Caudieux

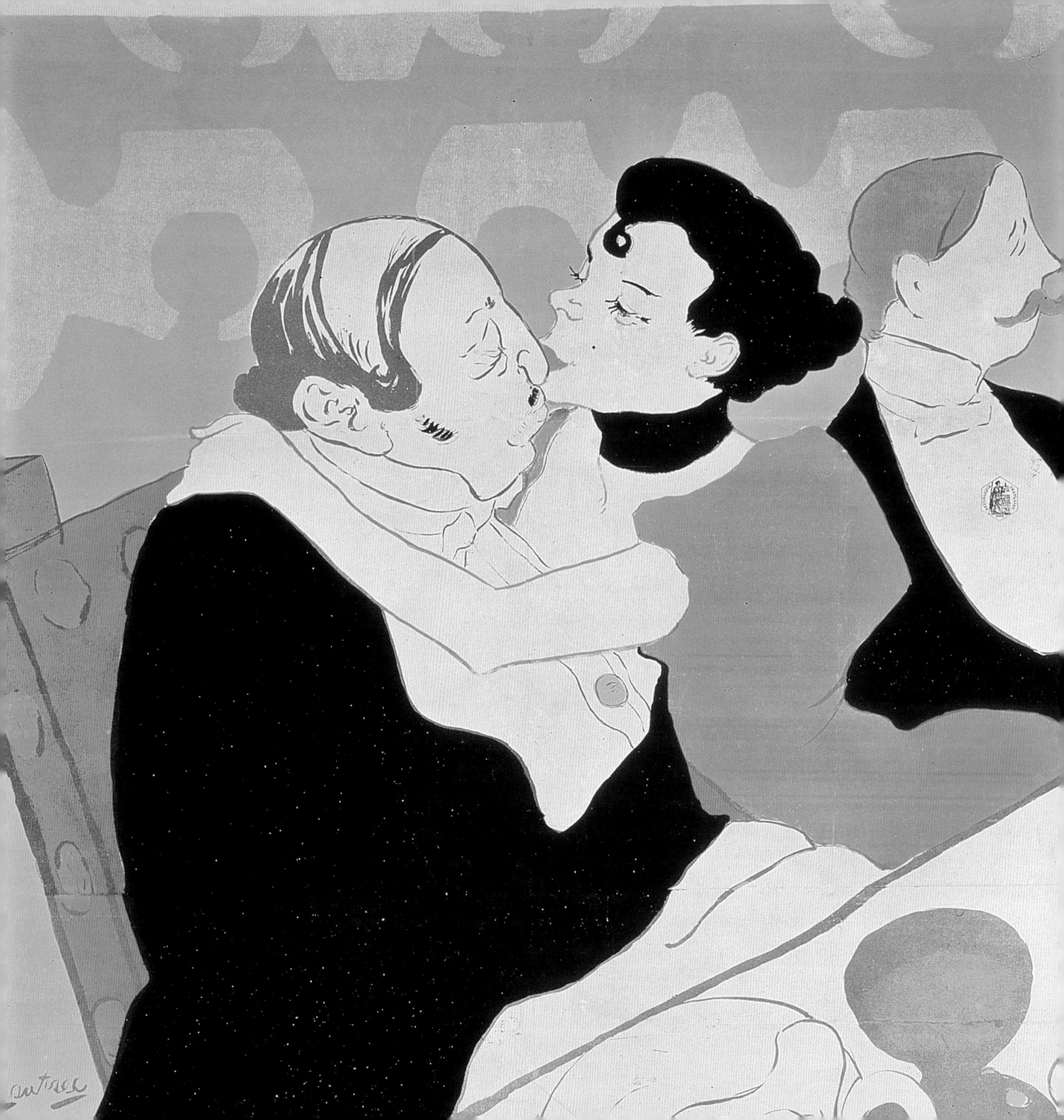

Director's Acknowledgements

Plate 5
(detail, opposite)
Henri
de Toulouse-Lautrec
(1864–1901)
Reine de Joie
1892
Colour lithograph,
136 x 92 cm
Bridgeman Art Library/Private Collection
An example was shown at the London poster exhibition 1894–5, No. 126 [40/- or £2]

For many Britons, their first glimpse of the work of Toulouse-Lautrec and other modern French artists may have come with a huge exhibition of posters held in London in the years 1894–95. This exhibition, held not in an art gallery but in an entertainment centre or music hall called the 'Royal Aquarium', was widely reviewed and hugely successful. The exhibition was so well received that the organizers were induced to hold a second exhibition in 1896. Though catalogues for the exhibitions were published and survive in many public institutions, the exhibitions as a whole had been largely forgotten until the Victoria and Albert Museum exhibition *The Power of the Poster* in 1998. This exhibition drew attention to the importance of the exhibition of 1894–95 and the fact that many of the posters themselves had survived in the Victoria and Albert Museum as the gift of Mrs. Joseph Thacher Clarke, the widow of one of the original organizers. Through the kindness of the Victoria and Albert Museum, and a research grant from the British Library through the North East Museums, Libraries and Archives Council, it has been possible to resurrect much of the exhibition and the British response to it.

We are most grateful to Margaret Timmers, Curator of Posters at the Word and Image department of the Victoria and Albert Museum for suggesting this exhibition, and to her colleagues Janet Skidmore and Ruth Hibbard for organizing the loan itself. We are also grateful to Meryl Huxtable, Mike Wheeler, and Mark Sandiford for their work on the conservation of these fragile items. At The Bowes Museum I am grateful to Margaret's former colleague Howard Coutts, and Claire Jones for researching and writing the catalogue. I am also grateful to Jane Whittaker, Vivien Reid, Vincent Shawcross, and Roy Wood for their practical skills in organizing and mounting the exhibition. The design of the catalogue and exhibition panels was carried out with his usual enthusiasm by Trevor Hatchett of Barron Hatchett Design, with photographs of items from The Bowes Museum supplied by Syd Neville.

Our exhibition programme is supported by Northern Rock and the Friends of The Bowes Museum, whose help is vital to help us achieve an international dimension to our exhibitions, with the help of Durham County Council, who provide core funding for the museum.

Adrian Jenkins
Director

Toulouse-Lautrec and the Art of the French Poster

"How much Paris is ahead of us may now be clearly perceived at the Aquarium, where all the more striking Parisian posters are on view. A vast amount of talent, and even genius, is expended on these things. They are carrying decorative art towards new boundaries."

Newcastle Daily Leader, 25 October, 1894

THE POSTER was a relatively new art form when the first English exhibition of posters opened in London in 1894.[1] Pictorial posters had developed in France in the second half of the nineteenth century through the medium of lithography, a flat or 'planographic' printing process whereby a design drawn in greasy pen on a smooth stone is transferred onto many separate sheets of paper. The effect is often like that of a chalk drawing, with subtleties in the shadows and nuances of tone which had not been so easily obtainable in other printing processes. In its early days, lithography was seen largely as a means of reproducing existing images, but it soon developed into an expressive medium in its own right. French artists such as Théodore Géricault (1791–1824) and Eugène Delacroix (1798–1863) produced sombre and powerful images, the latter for book illustrations for *Faust* (1828) and *Hamlet* (1844).

Colour lithography was developed from the 1830s. Here, a different stone for each colour had to be precisely aligned one after another during the printing processes. The process depended on the use of a registration frame developed by Godefroy Engelmann in 1837, and utilised the three primary colours of red, blue and yellow, printed over a basic outline or composition of black to give underlying shadows and depth. Masterpieces of colour lithography included Thomas Shotter Boys' *Picturesque Architecture in Paris, Ghent and Rouen* of 1839. However, the process was extremely expensive and did not entirely replace colouring by hand as a means of producing coloured prints.

By mid-century colour lithography was more generally available, most obviously in the form of printed music covers. These covers made the music visually attractive to a general audience. The main producer seems to have been England, which produced a huge number of covers alluding to the title of the music, though almost invariably of minor artistic importance (PLATE 6). Meanwhile, in France, lithography was used by the great caricaturists Paul Gavarni (1804–1866) and Honoré Daumier (1808–1879) for prints in satirical publications such as *Le Charivari*. Though these were mass-produced commercial publications, the artistic quality of their work was widely recognized at the time (PLATE 7).

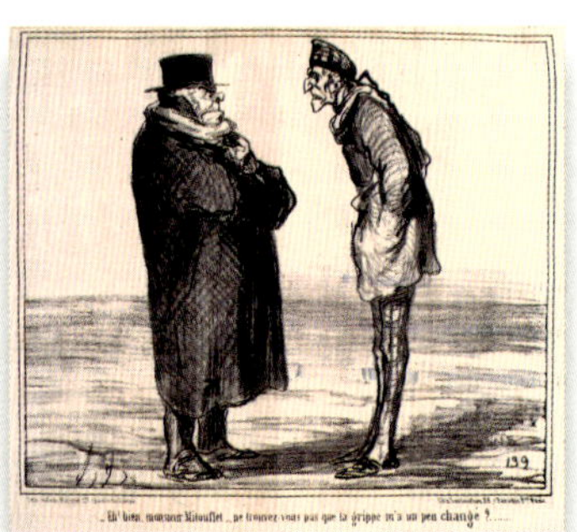

Plate 6* *(opposite)
W. Spalding & T. Packer
Les Sirènes (The Sirens)
ENGLISH, NINETEENTH CENTURY
COLOUR LITHOGRAPH
34.5 X 25.4 CM
Private collection

Plate 7* *(below left)
Honoré Daumier (1808–1879)
Eh! bien, monsieur Mitouflet... ne trouvez-vous pas que la grippe m'a un peu changé? (Well, Mr.Mitouflet, don't you think that the flu has altered my appearance?)
CARICATURE FROM *LE CHARIVARI*, 25 JANUARY 1858
25.4 X 36.5 CM
The Bowes Museum

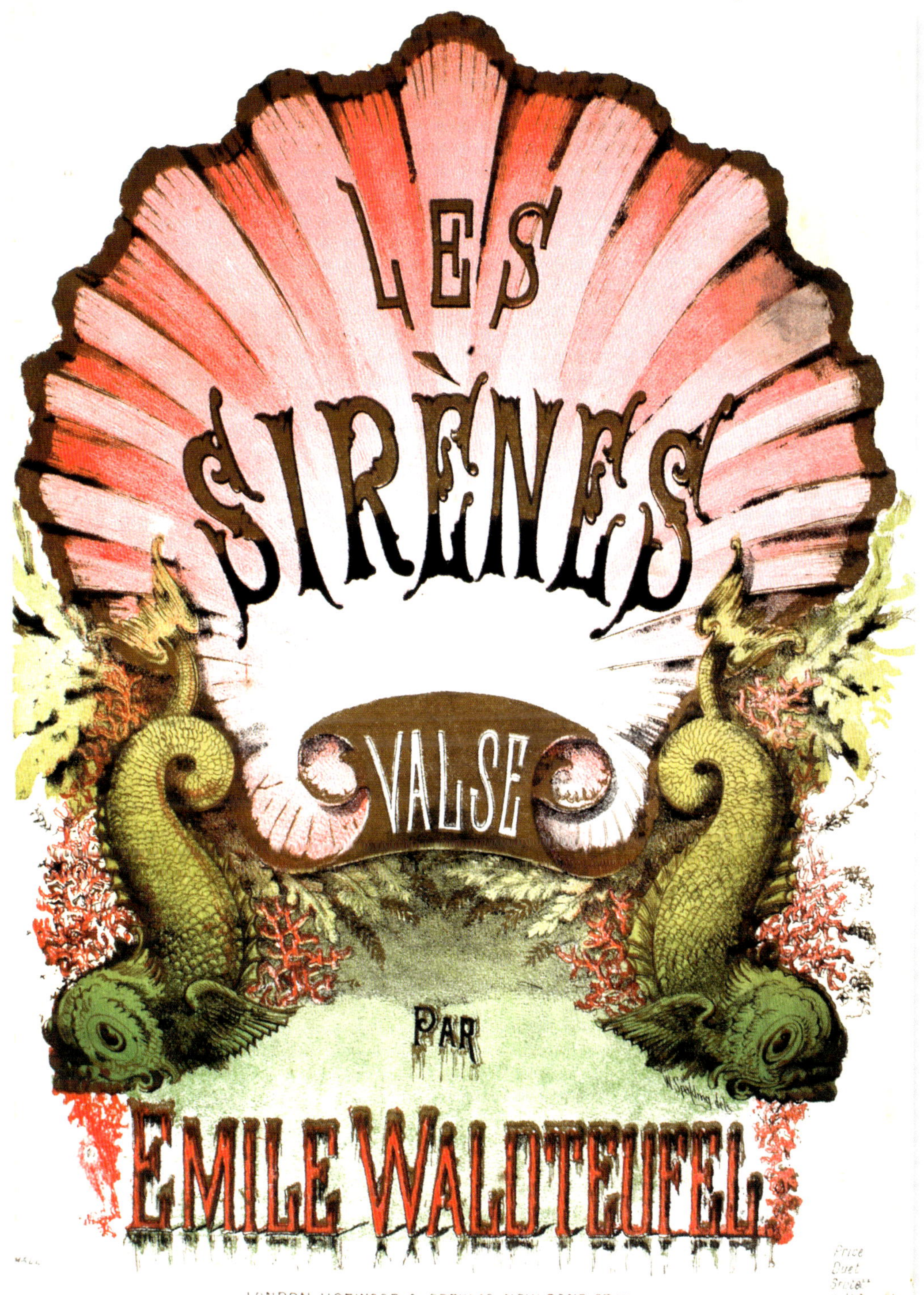
LES
SIRÈNES
VALSE
PAR
EMILE WALDTEUFEL
Price
Duet
LONDON HOPWOOD & CREW, 42 NEW BOND S^T W

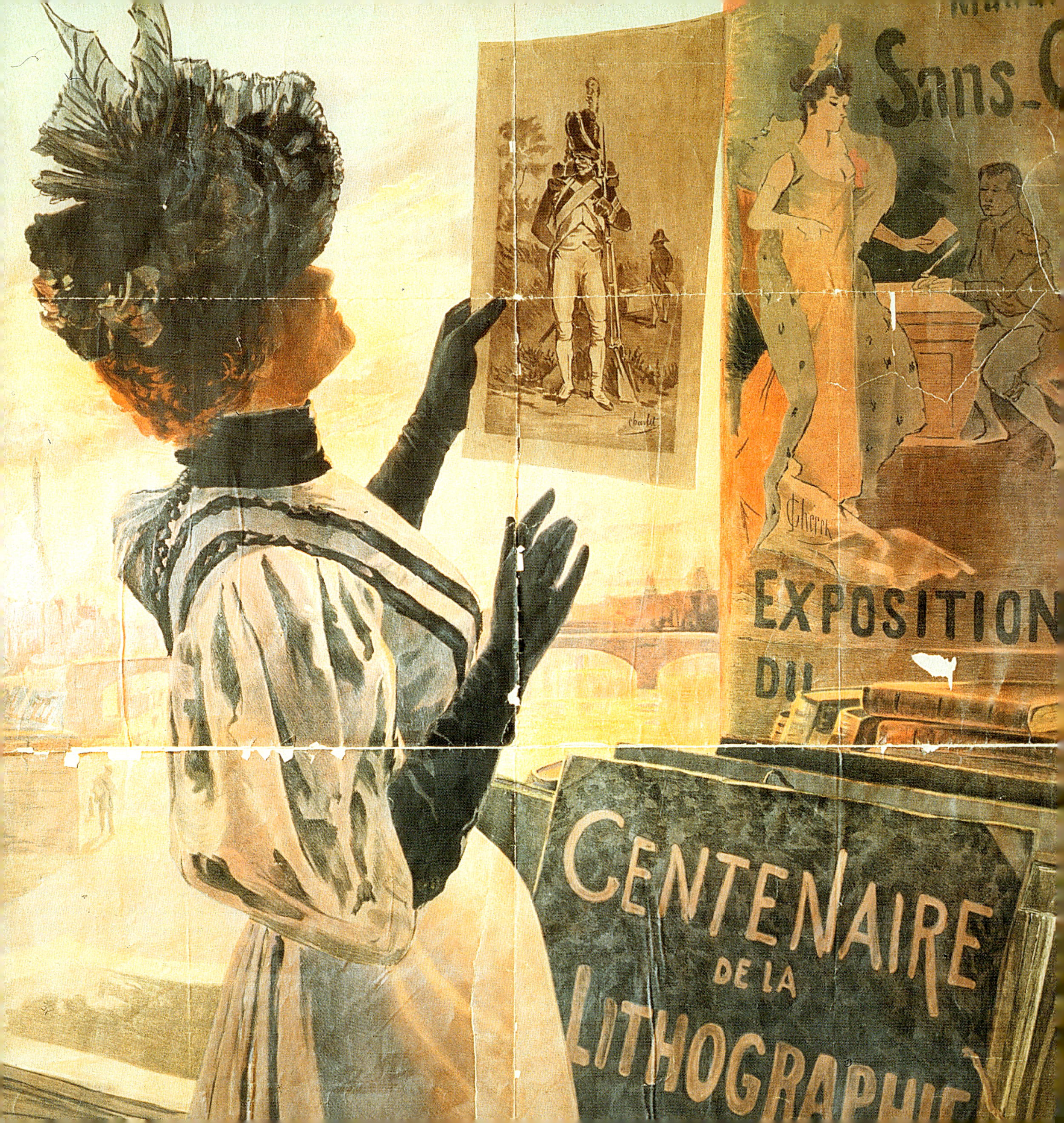
EXPOSITION
DU
CENTENAIRE
DE LA
LITHOGRAPHIE

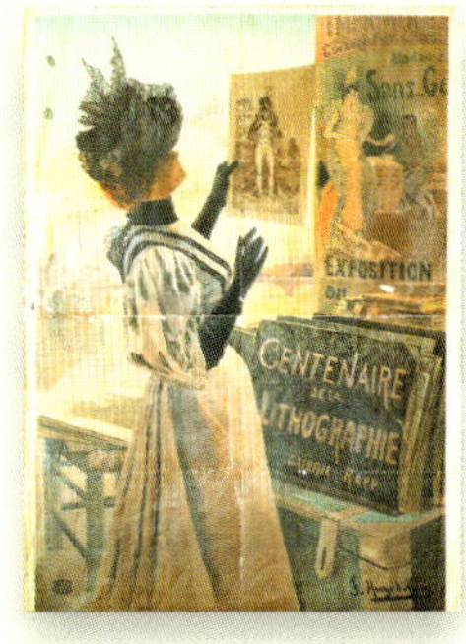

Plate 8
(above & detail left)
F. Hugo d'Alési
(1849–1906)
Exposition du Centenaire de la Lithographie, Galérie Rapp
1895
Colour lithograph
150.5 x 107cm
V&A Images/Victoria & Albert Museum
An example was shown at the London poster exhibition 1896, No. 61 (seven colours) or No. 62 (six colours) (10/- or 50p)
The poster in the background is Chéret's 'Madame Sans-Gêne'

A great stride for the commercial and artistic use of lithography came mid century with the development of a large printing press that could print from large stones. This produced large images in great quantity, and led to the development of the advertising poster (PLATE 8). These could either be printed on a large sheet of paper, or be composed of several sheets of paper pasted together to form one huge design.

Until the mid-nineteenth century the design of the poster had been mainly limited to different styles of lettering obtained from the medium of letter press. These were posted over hoardings and walls both in France and England. Some survive for such subjects as theatrical performances and sporting events, with the names of the protagonists given in different type. Sometimes a woodcut or wood-engraved image could be added to add interest (PLATE 9). In England posters seem to have been particularly prevalent on hoardings connected with demolitions in the city of London where so much was being rebuilt. In France, particularly in Paris, small round circular illuminated pavilions or 'kiosks' had been designed for the display of posters, and formed a characteristic feature of the Parisian street scene noted by visitors from abroad. These became ubiquitous after a law of 1881 allowed the more general placing of posters, providing they were on tinted paper, had paid a tax, and had a special stamp affixed[2] (PLATE 3).

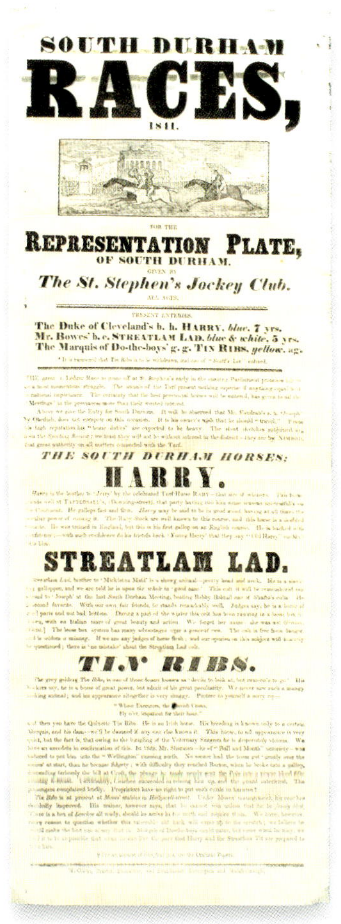

Plate 9 (right)
Poster advertising the South Durham races
woodcut and letterpress 1841
50.5 x 18.5 cm

By the 1880s a handful of posters were printed in colour by means of colour lithography, using standard representational images of the time.

The development of the poster as an art form was due entirely to one man: the French lithographer Jules Chéret (1836–1932). He transformed the poster almost overnight – or at least in the space of a very few years – from being at the best a colourful but garish means of advertising a product, through to something that expressed the values and innovations of French art and society of the second half of the nineteenth century. He combined this with a sure commercial acumen, and his posters always attracted attention to the product. Chéret is justifiably seen as the father of the modern poster both as an art and as an advertising form.

Chéret began his career in 1858 with a poster for Offenbach's opera *Orpheus in the Underworld*. This proved to be a false start, as it led to no further commissions of this sort. He then went to London, where he produced lithographed showcards, brochures and a letter heading for the perfumier Eugène Rimmel, who financed Chéret's own printing firm for his return to Paris in 1866. Chéret was able to set up his own firm with the new large lithographic presses that were being developed in London, and preferred to work directly on the lithographic stones. Having sold the production side of his firm to the firm of Chaix in 1881, he was free to devote himself to the designing of posters that came to dominate the Parisian street scene. He was to produce over two thousand poster designs in all.

Chéret's posters show knowledge of developments in French painting, in that they imitate in lithographic form the free and easy brushstrokes and light effects of Impressionist painting. As they advertised contemporary products, they naturally illustrated contemporary Parisian life. They generally featured a pretty woman, scantily clad, who drew the passer-by's attention to what she was using – anything from lamp oil to throat pastilles. He preferred working on posters of the largest size of 248 x 88 cm because he could include the whole human figure. He was particularly distinguished for his use of reflected light, which he achieved through the subtlest of lithographic techniques, using a delicate overlay of colours. This was naturally most appropriate for those posters that related to the theatre, music halls and other places of entertainment (PLATE 10). These proliferated in late nineteenth century Paris, and attracted a broad patronage, including that of intellectuals and artists. The most famous were the *Moulin Rouge*, the *Elysée Montmartre*, and the *Chat Noir.* Here there was drinking, singing and dancing, and a meeting of different sections of society, especially working class women, and upper class men and tourists. This was despite the presence of a certain type of policeman whose job it was to make sure that everybody behaved, and the dancers dressed with decency!

Chéret's self-proclaimed artistic aim was to brighten up the streets of Paris, and in his work of the 1890s he deliberately restricted himself to a colourful but limited palette of the three primary colours – red, yellow and blue – with which he achieved effects that he compared to a 'nosegay' of flowers. His posters could be sold in different colour combinations, not only for the benefit of the advertiser, but also the collector of posters, who was becoming a major force at the time. One of the leading merchants was Sagot, who produced a catalogue, with a lithographed cover by Chéret, in 1891.

They also featured prominently in the magazine, *Les Maîtres de l'Affiche* – The Masters of the Poster – which in the years 1896 to 1900 reproduced small versions of famous posters, with an added original lithograph by a famous designer as a bonus.

Chéret was awarded the *Légion d'Honneur* in 1889 for creating 'a branch of art, by applying art to commercial and industrial printing'. His work was much imitated by other poster artists and graphic designers and is in many ways responsible for creating the image of Paris as a city of entertainment and pleasure that has survived into the present day.

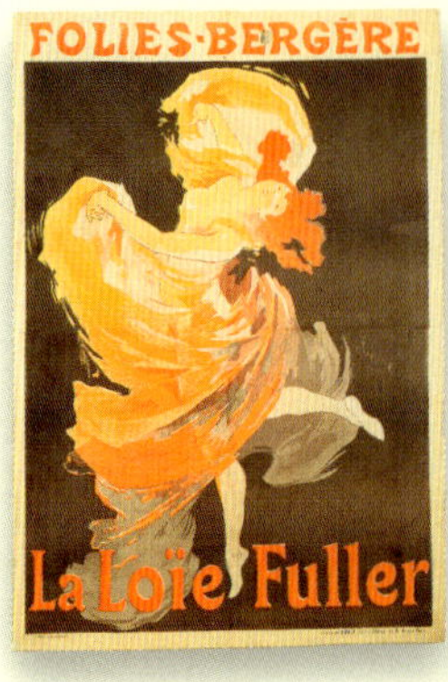

Plate 10
(above & detail, right)
Jules Chéret
(1836–1932)
Folies-Bergère:
La Loïe Fuller
Colour lithograph
120 x 82 cm
V&A Images/Victoria & Albert Museum
An example was shown at the London poster exhibition 1894–5, No. 51 (40/- or £2 for a set of four)

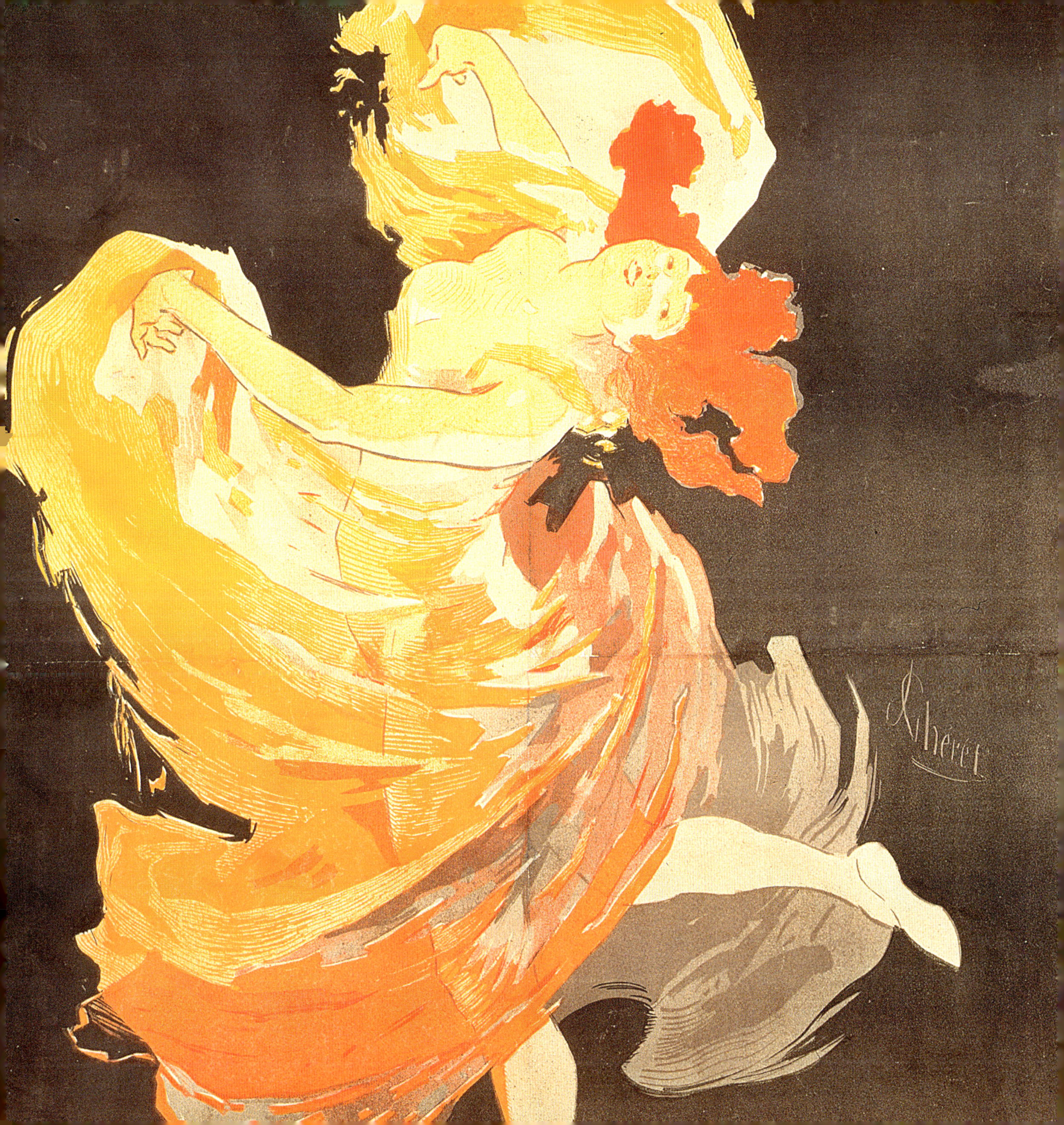

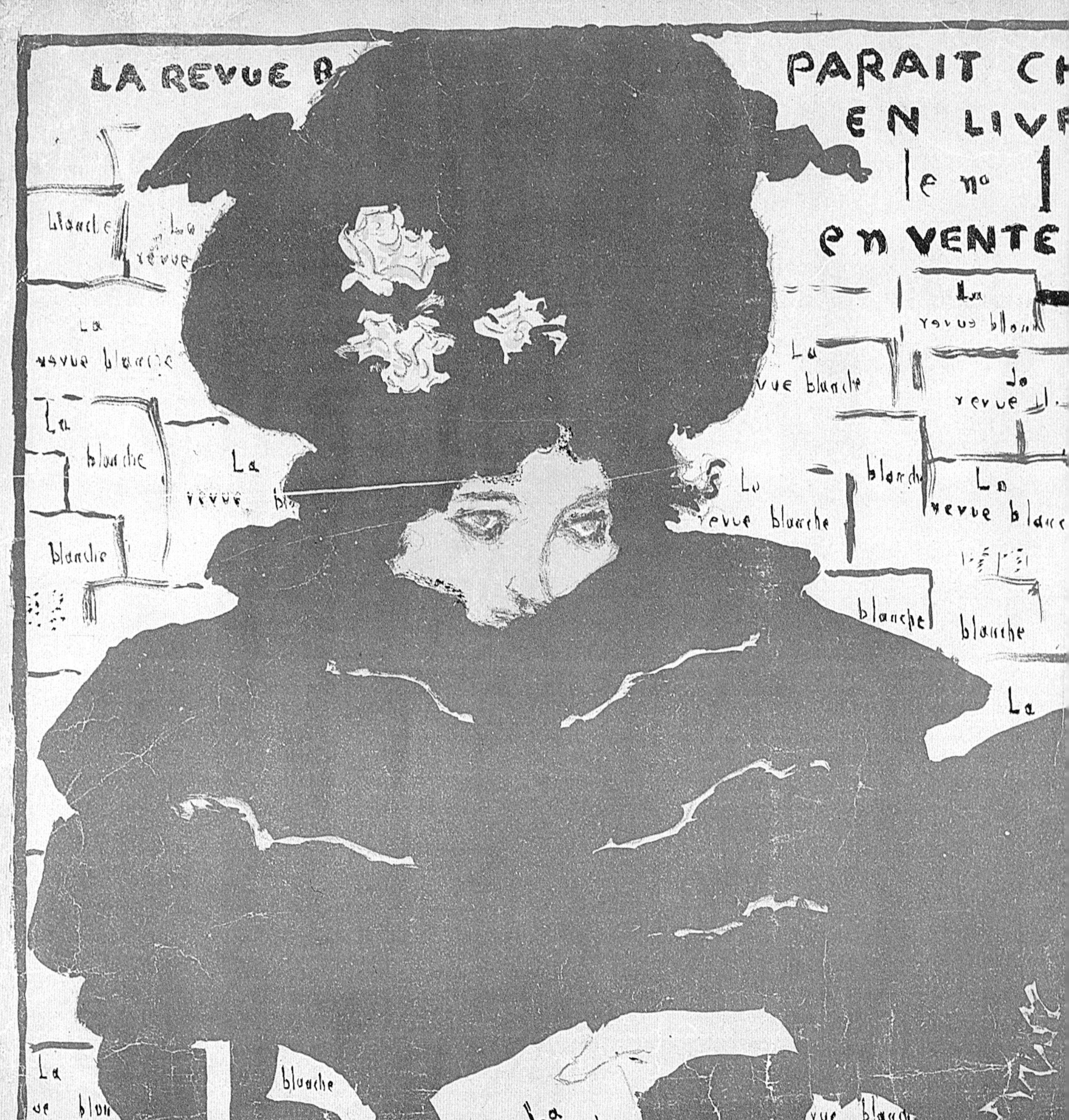
LA REVUE B
PARAIT CH
EN LIV
le no 1
en VENTE
La revue blanche

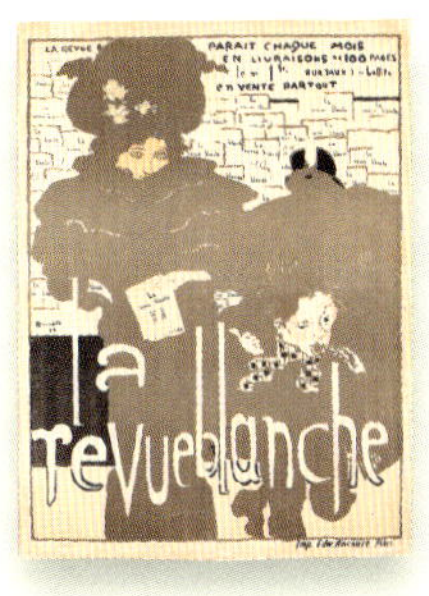

Plate 11
(above & detail, left)
Pierre Bonnard
(1867–1947)
La Revue Blanche
1894
Colour lithograph
83 x 63.5 cm
V&A Images/Victoria & Albert Museum
An example was shown at the London poster exhibition 1894–5, No. 11 (7/- or 35p)

Plate 12 (right)
Japanese woodblock print
Probably bought by Joséphine Bowes in Paris in the period 1862–74
36.5 x 25 cm
The Bowes Museum

Chéret's artistic inspiration perhaps gained its first adherent in the work of the artist Pierre Bonnard (1867–1947). In his poster *France Champagne* of 1891, Bonnard showed he had grasped one of the basic principles of advertising, selling a product by means of a pretty woman, but brought his own inspiration to bear. He also contributed a more complex poster for a modern art periodical called *La Revue Blanche* (The White Review) showing a woman in fashionable dress in the street, portrayed in an asymmetrical, angular style characteristic of advanced art of the time (PLATE 11).

However, the greatest figure that emerged from the revolution initiated by Chéret was the artist Henri de Toulouse-Lautrec (1864–1901).[3] Lautrec is of course known today for his images of the Parisian music hall and night life (or 'café concerts' or singing cafés as the English called them), but particularly for his incisive line and acute observation, akin to Daumier's talent for caricature.

Lautrec was born of noble family in 1864 in Albi in southern France. Early on he showed signs of being a talented artist and caricaturist. He studied at the studio of the established painter Fernand Cormon (1854–1924) in Paris in 1883–84, but found himself increasingly attracted to more modern art, especially the work of the French Impressionists, headed by Manet and Degas.

His early paintings are portraits and scenes with horses. However, during the 1880s and 1890s he came increasingly to portray the life of the music halls and 'cabarets' (drinking bars) in his beloved Montmartre in northern Paris, where he had a studio. Many of his paintings depict scenes of this world, particularly the dance halls and bars where singers entertained.

In the 1890s Lautrec became thoroughly familiar with the medium of lithography, and had produced book illustrations and independent prints in colour and black and white which showed his supreme mastery of the medium. His main source of artistic inspiration here was the Japanese woodblock illustrations that were highly prized in France, whose visual effect depended on large blocks of colour in the design, without any great attempt at overall perspective (PLATE 12).

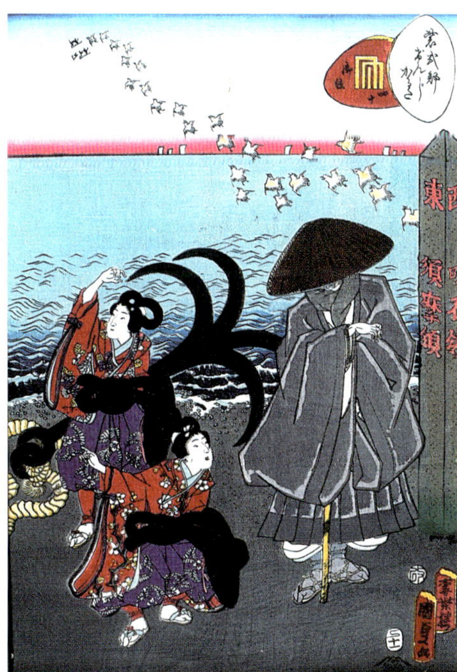

In 1891 Lautrec produced his first poster, a design for the music hall the *Moulin Rouge* (Red Windmill) featuring the well-known profiles of the dancers *La Goulue* (the glutton) and *Valentin le Désossé* (the boneless one). The lettering, like Chéret's, is part of the design, the repeated 'M' perhaps echoing the letter press advertisements in newspapers.

This poster was rapidly followed by one for the dancer Jane Avril (PLATE 20), another for the comedian Caudieux (PLATE4), and a famous series for the singer and entertainer Aristide Bruant (PLATE 29). Bruant was famous for his attacks on his middle and upper class audience, and for his use of working class idioms and *argot* (slang). He commissioned a number of posters from Lautrec, and refused to perform if they were not shown, despite the objections of the cabaret owner, who found them too bizarre.

By the late 1890s Lautrec was exhausted, physically and mentally, by his dissolute way of living. He returned to his earlier fascination with animals and caricature. He died in 1901, leaving a body of work which seems to sum up Paris life of the 1890s.

One artist who rejected a poster by Lautrec was the singer Yvette Guilbert, who was unwilling to be portrayed as a caricature across Paris, although she did allow Lautrec to produce a book of lithographs in her honour. She was happier to be portrayed by the Swiss artist Théophile-Alexandre Steinlen (1859–1923), who had come to Paris in 1880 and began as a lithographer, producing designs for wallpaper and textiles. He was famous for his interest in Parisian types and working class life, as well as his love of cats, which featured in much of his work (PLATE 30). He was also keen to portray human types as seen in the street, of which he kept a record. He said that *the Parisian poor are far more picturesque, both in bearing, clothing, expression and general characteristics, than their more prosperous brethren. The life of the café is also full of interest. I always try to place any types of which I make use in their own surroundings; and when I am ignorant of a certain 'milieu', I go out and seek for what I want till I find it.* [4]

Another artist who turned his attention to the poster was Eugène Grasset (1841–1917) who was already known as a designer, especially of stained glass windows in the medieval tradition, before he began designing posters in 1886. He brought to posters characteristics of stained glass, such as flat areas of colour with strong outlining, and elaborate surface decoration. He is best known for his depictions of the great dramatic actress Sarah Bernhardt as Joan of Arc.

Other well known artists include Boutet de Monvel (1851–1913), Jean de Paleologue, otherwise known as *Pal* (1860–1942), Henri-Gabriel Ibels (1867–1936), Albert Guillaume (1873–1942) and Félix Vallotton (1865–1925). Many of these worked independently as illustrators and designers, producing work which featured Parisian types, sometimes to comic effect, sometimes with serious social intent. The best known poster designer of the later 1890s was the Czechoslovakian-born artist Alphonse Mucha (1860–1939). His first success was a poster of Sarah Bernhardt in the play *Gismonda* in 1895. His elaborate naturalistic imagery, with plants trailing over the design, made him one of the chief exponents of the *Art Nouveau* style of the years around 1900.

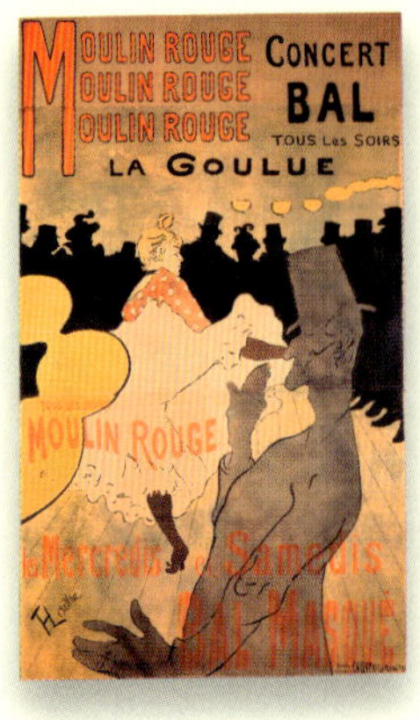

Plate 13
(above & detail, right)
Henri
de Toulouse-Lautrec
(1864–1901)
Moulin Rouge – La Goulue
1891
Colour lithograph
193 x 117 cm
Bridgeman Art Library
San Diego Museum of Art, USA
An example was shown at the London poster exhibition 1894–5, No. 120 (80/- or £4)

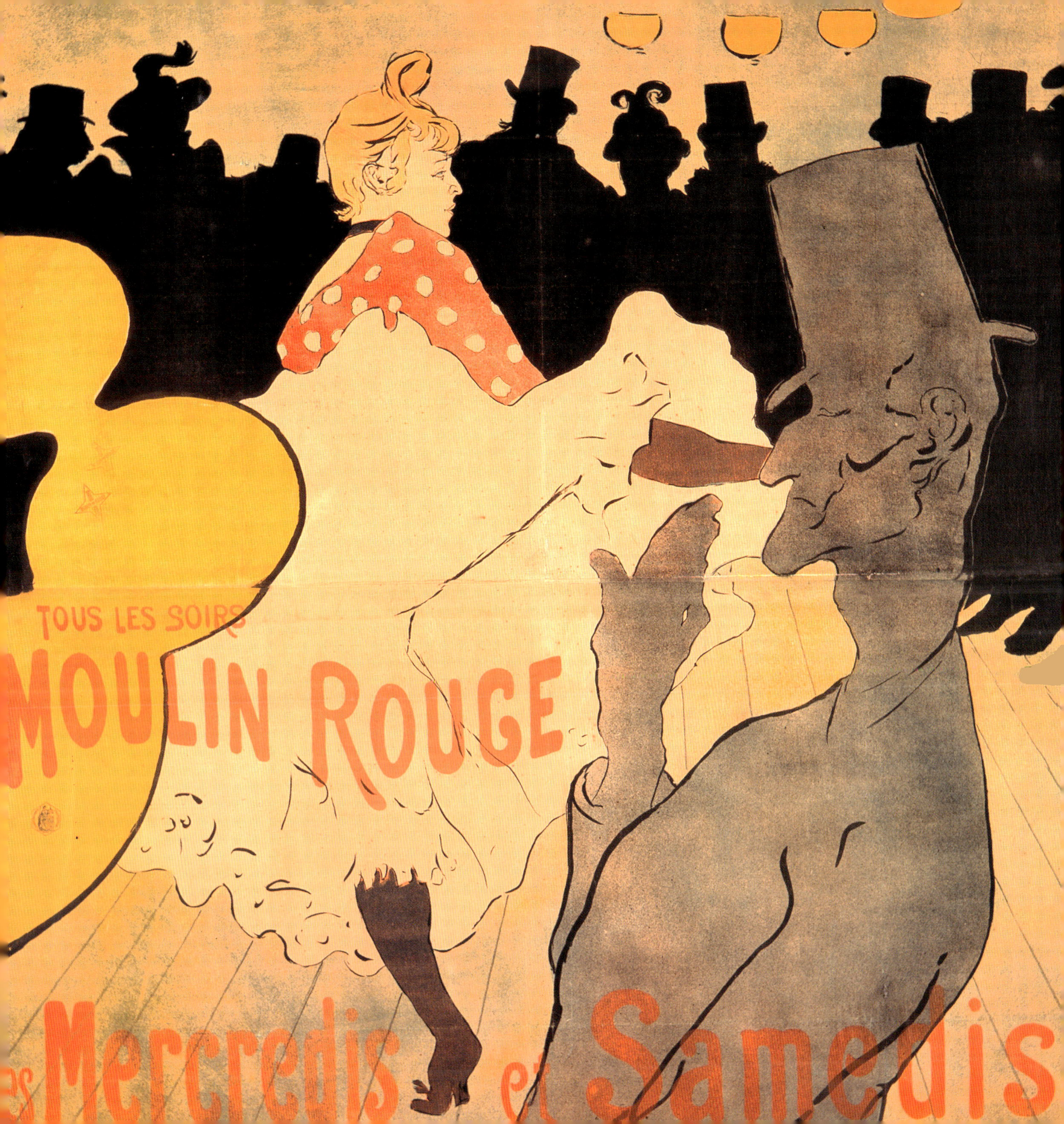
TOUS LES SOIRS
MOULIN ROUGE
es Mercredis et Samedis

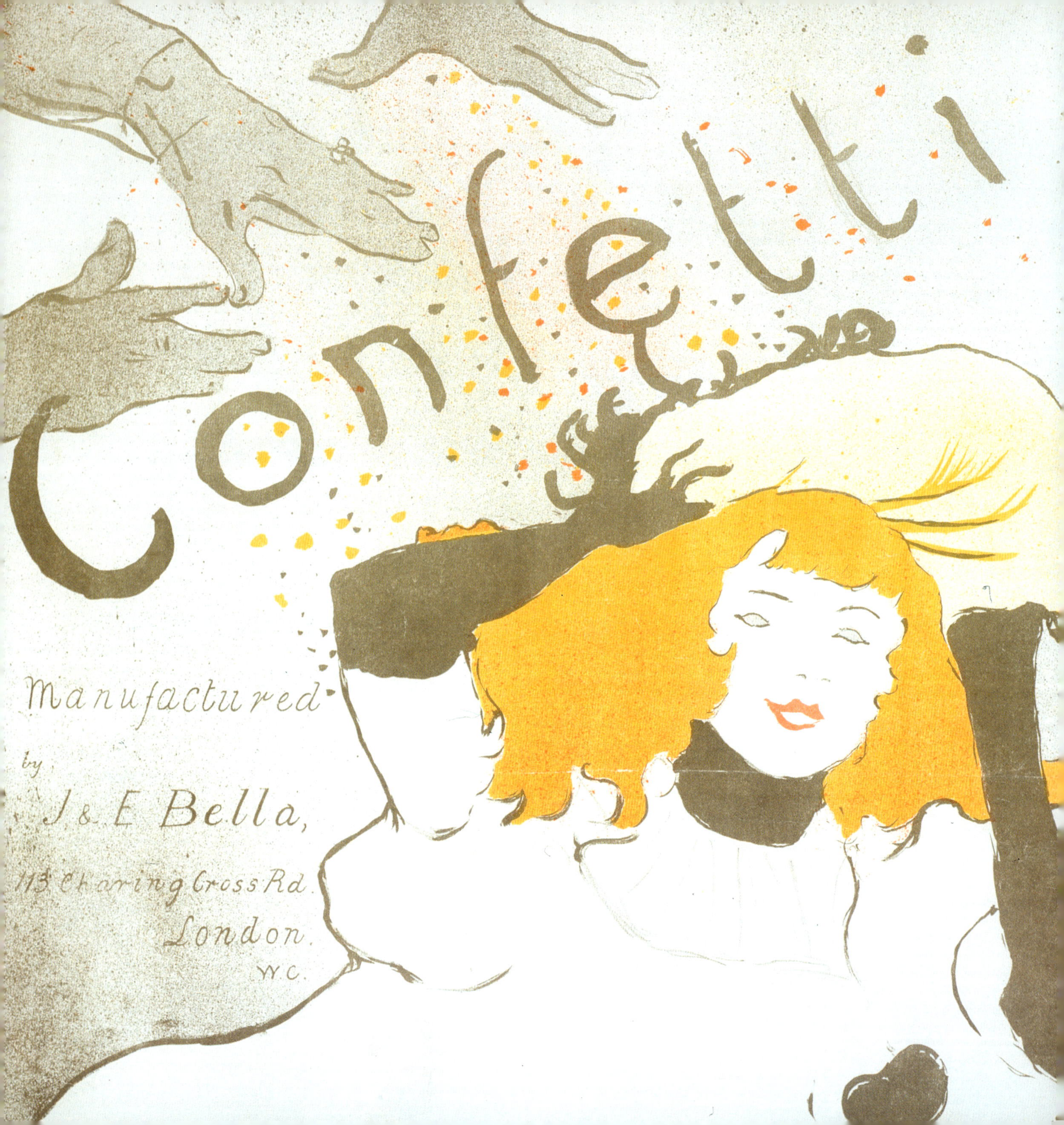
Confetti
Manufactured
by
J. & E. Bella,
113 Charing Cross Rd.
London.
W.C.

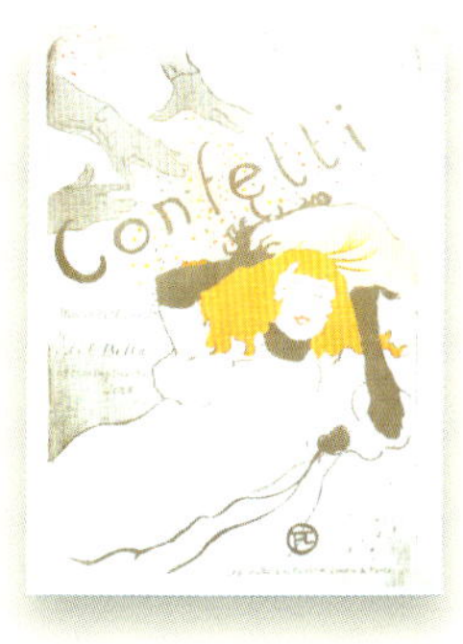

Plate 14
(above & detail, left)
Henri
de Toulouse-Lautrec
(1864–1901)
Confetti
1894
COLOUR LITHOGRAPH
61 X 46 CM
V&A Images/Victoria & Albert Museum
An example was shown at the London poster exhibition 1894–5, No. 130 (4/- or 20p). Edward Bella commissioned this poster from Lautrec and used it as the frontispiece to the catalogue of the first exhibition of posters in London in 1894. Lautrec came to London for the exhibition.

It is not easy to say when the British first became aware of the poster phenomenon in France. Britain had already had its first poster artist of significance, with Fred Walker's design for *The Woman in White*, a well known design of 1871 that predates most French pictorial posters by several years. The great British contribution – if such it can be called – was for a commercial manufacturer to buy a painting by a distinguished artist and to use it as a commercial publicity image. This happened famously with Millais' painting of *Bubbles*, an image of a little boy blowing soap bubbles, which became an advertisement for Pears Soap. The reproductions were miracles of exact colour lithography, but had little merit as independent works of art.

The poster as a potential art form had been discussed in England as early as 1881, when *The Magazine of Art* published an article entitled 'The Street as Art Galleries'. In 1893 it published an article on Chéret by Robert H. Sherard, while *The Studio* published an article by Charles Hiatt entitled 'The Collecting of Posters: A New Field for Connoisseurs' which discusses the poster as a new field in collecting. He discussed not only Chéret, but also Willette and Vallotton, and the tone of these articles makes it clear that quite a few Englishmen had been over to Paris and were aware of the developments in the French poster. *The Studio* had been published that year as a glossy art magazine with 'advanced' tendencies that left *The Magazine of Art* and other periodicals somewhat in the shade. Deliberately international in scope, it was not afraid to discuss and illustrate modern work from abroad, though it tended to avoid the more controversial and avant-garde works being executed in France and elsewhere on the Continent.

It was in this context that the first public exhibition of posters was held in London in 1894. It was organized by an exceptionally enterprising printer, Edward Bella, who had offices in both London and Paris, in partnership with the Frenchman de Malherbe. He was clearly alive to developments in French art, and contributed an article on English posters to the French periodical *La Plume*. He had even commissioned a poster from Lautrec, *Confetti*, which formed the frontispiece to the catalogue (PLATE 14). Lautrec's letters show that he actually came over for the exhibition.[5] However, Bella had turned for a venue not to an established art gallery, but to an entertainment centre and music hall of somewhat dubious repute, called the 'Royal Aquarium'.

The Royal Aquarium in London stood where the Methodist Central Hall now stands in Westminster. It had been erected in 1876 as a kind of public entertainment centre, with (naturally) a series of fish tanks as some of its main attractions. In 1886 it was stated that it *consists of a large Hall, about 340 feet long, by about 158 feet wide, and 32 feet high, and an annexe at the Eastern End, about 136 feet long, 80 feet wide, and 32 feet high. The Western portion of the Premises* [was] *formerly known as the Imperial Theatre.* Around the hall on the first floor was a gallery or 'promenade', where the poster exhibitions were held. The fish tanks did not last very long, though exhibitions of swimming and diving continued until the venue closed in 1903.

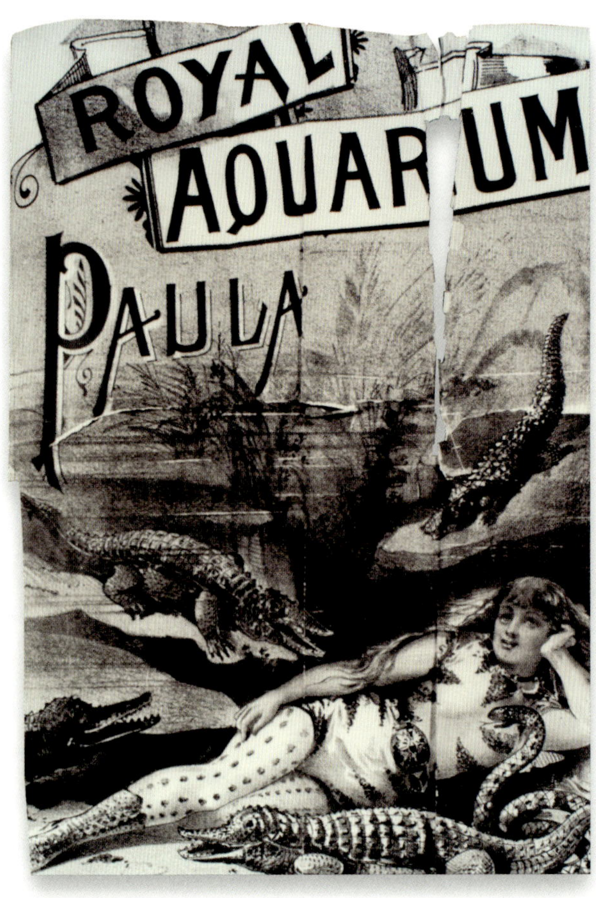

The Royal Aquarium had already been associated in the public mind with posters in 1890, when it had been the centre of a huge row or scandal. It had displayed a large poster of a female acrobat, Zaeo, which portrayed her in a pose and clothes that were seen by some as too revealing (PLATE 16). This poster, very much a forerunner of seaside postcards or even *Carry On* films, caused outrage among certain members of the community. Given the proximity to Westminster Abbey, it was perhaps unavoidable that various clerics and others wrote to protest about it.

As a place of entertainment the Royal Aquarium had to be licensed by the newly formed London County Council. Their deliberations on the affair are recorded in a volume in the London Metropolitan Archives.[6] In addition, the case was widely reported in the national press and got the Aquarium a reputation for sensationalism and controversial posters.

The first reference comes on 21 May, 1890, with a complaint about *pictorial advertisements (issued by the managers of certain places of entertainment) which disgrace the hoardings of the streets of London.* The rumpus continued into August and September, when William Alexander Coote, Secretary of the National Vigilance Society, wrote to object to *certain wall posters or placards of Zaeo and Paula* (PLATES 15 & 16), as well as to a book or pamphlet containing four photographs of Zaeo in different postures, which were alleged to be of an objectionable character. An article in *The Daily Telegraph*, 23 May, 1890, under 'Police Intelligence' refers to *a young lady without much clothing on.* The paper reported that Mr. Coote objected to the emphasis on her bust and thighs, stating that *so dexterously has the picture been drawn that as men of the world, Londoners must be led to the conviction that this lady actually appeared in*

Plate 15
(left)
Poster of 'Paula'
1890
LITHOGRAPH
London Metropolitan Archives
(LCC/MIN/10,891)

Plate 16
(right)
Letter regarding the 'Zaeo' poster for the Royal Aquarium
London Metropolitan Archives
(LCC/MIN/10,891)

Plate 17
(far right)
Souvenir publication of the 'Zaeo' affair
Published by the Royal Aquarium
1891
London Metropolitan Archives
(LCC/MIN/10,891)

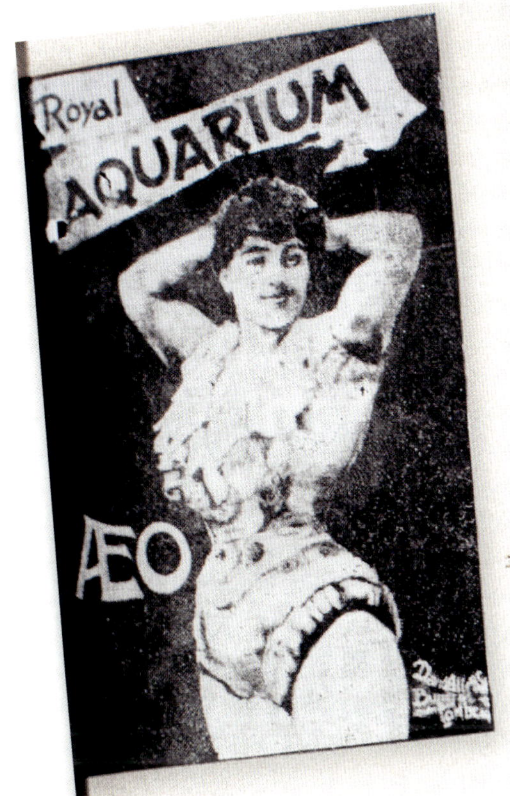

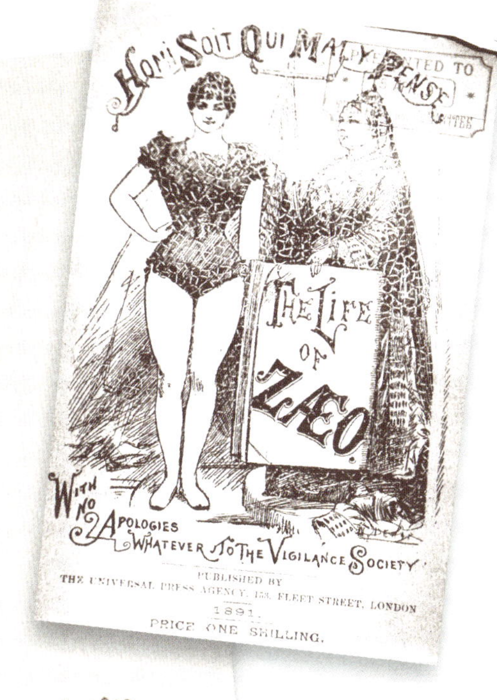

200, EUSTON ROAD,
LONDON, N.W.,
September 29th, 1890.

SIR,

The above sketch is a photograph from a huge street advertisement, copies of which are to be found on most London street hoardings, and also on some street hoardings in the provinces, notably in the vicinity of Brighton. The question in the minds of many persons is, Will a new licence be granted to the advertisers? The case rests absolutely on the vote of the London County Council at the coming Brewster Sessions.

I am, Sir,

Yours faithfully,

EDWARD W. THOMAS.

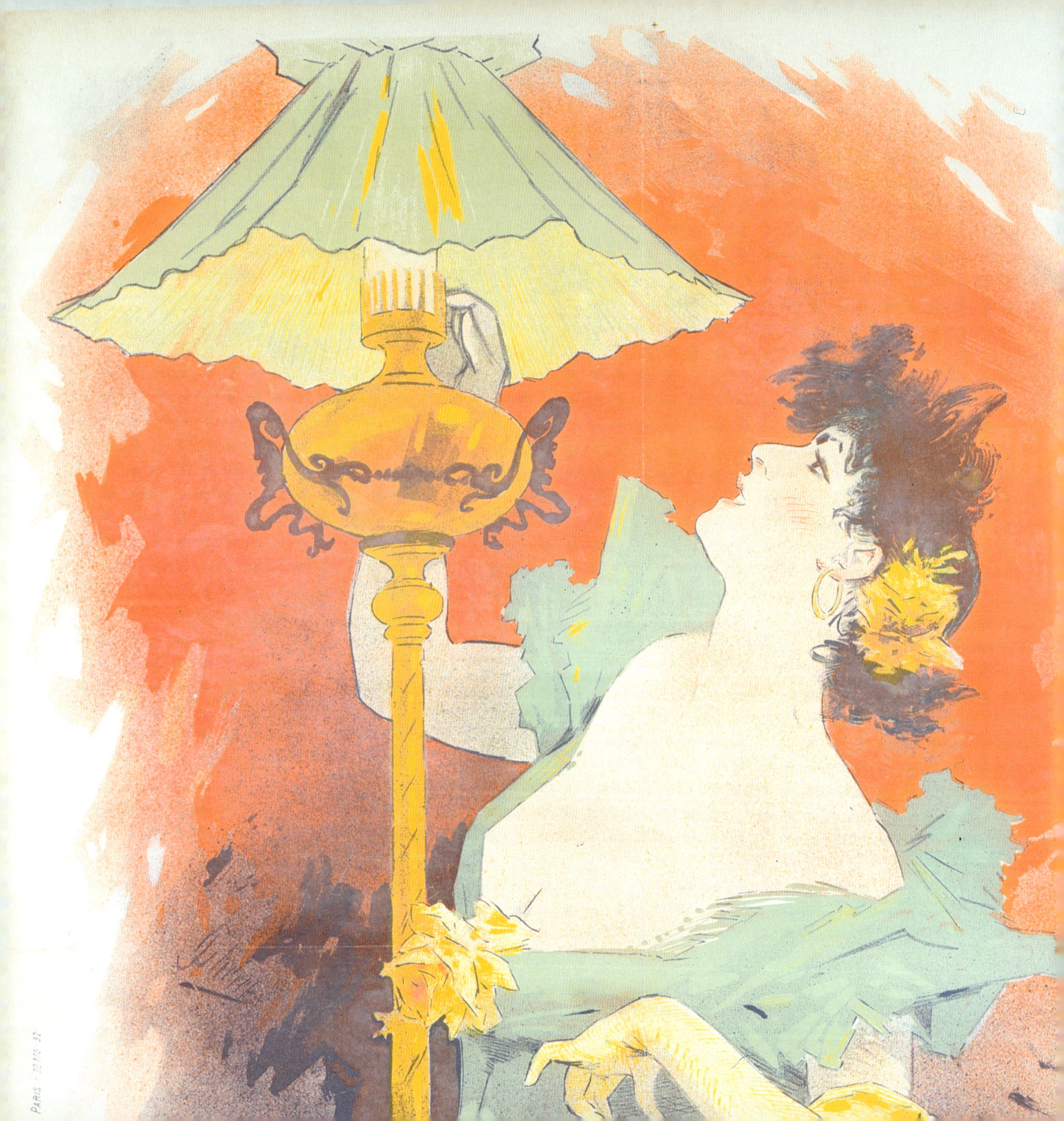
PARIS

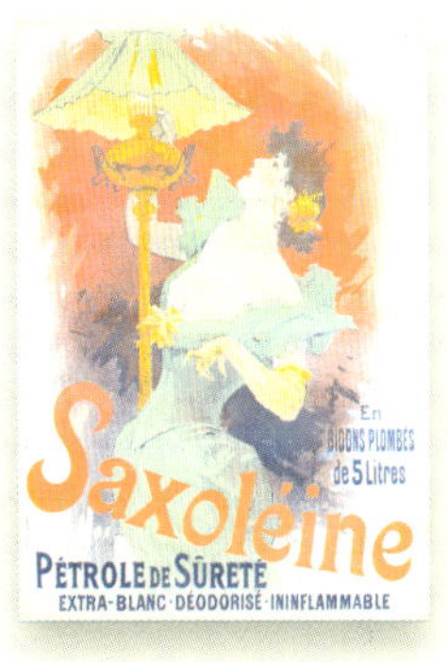

Plate 18 (above, & detail, left)
Jules Chéret (1836–1932)
Saxoléine: Pétrole de Sûreté
Colour lithograph
120 x 86 cm
V&A Images/Victoria & Albert Museum
An example was shown at the London poster exhibition 1894–5, No. 48 (5/ or 25p)

the same nude condition. The Committee made the renewal of the Aquarium's licence conditional on the exclusion of prostitutes and of this poster, as well as the banning of pamphlets and postcards showing it. These were thought to have vanished from public view, but thankfully specimens were bound in the records kept by the licensing committee (the Theatre and Music Hall Committee) of London County Council, and give us an idea of what the fuss was about. *The Times* noted that receipts to 30 June at the Aquarium totalled £12,790 7s 8d, though *needless to say, many of these people have been disappointed – except such as went to see a bona fide gymnastic performance, for there is nothing in Zaeo's dress to which anyone, short of those who put trousers on the legs of their pianos, need object.*[7]

The Zaeo affair was still fresh in people's minds when the exhibition of posters opened at the Aquarium in October 1894. It was alluded to in the preface of the catalogue by Joseph Thacher Clarke, one of the organizing committee, who noted the 'fitness of choice' of the Royal Aquarium, due to the fame of posters of 'Zaeo and her Modest Costume'. It is not clear whether the Zaeo poster was on view or not, though there appears to have been a selection from the Aquarium itself. The exhibition comprised over two hundred posters by French and English artists, mostly lent by the honorary committee. In addition to Clarke himself, this comprised G. R. Halkett, Ernest Hart, M.D., A. S. Hartrick, F. G. Prange, L. Ravenhill, Gleeson White, Victor Champier and F. G. Dumas. These were all recognized names in the art world of the day, Gleeson White being the editor of *The Studio.* Archibald Standish Hartrick was a friend of Lautrec's from his days in Cormon's studio, and lent many of his posters. Clarke's widow later gave the posters her husband lent, to the Victoria and Albert Museum in 1921. Some of them still retain the paper numbers pasted onto the bottom left from the exhibition of 1894–95.

In his preface, Clarke stressed the importance of the poster:

... to those who study the tendencies of our modern modes of artistic expression, it has for some years been evident that in no other branch of design the most characteristic features of everyday life find clearer and more drastic utterance than in the art of pictorial and mural advertisements... the most unaffected and typical artistic predilections of the Man in the Street can be best appreciated by a review of these striking works of line and colour, providing us with an unconscious and unimpeachable witness to the present status of our civilisation... the finest posters are, indeed, not only examples of artistic originality, beauty and excellence in technique, but actual records of the daily life and interests of the age. Clarke also wrote appreciations of Chéret, Lautrec and other French artists that are still valid today.

What was remarkable about the Aquarium display was the thoroughness with which it covered the poster medium, and with a selection that is still valid today. A contemporary review in *The Daily News* noted that *it may be stated that the exhibition comprises some hundreds of posters, including fifty of the best productions of Jules Chéret* (PLATE 18), *who may be called the father of the latter day poster, and the whole of the Buttes Chaumont series* (PLATE 19)*, the Saxoléine series, the principal Jardin de Paris, Horloge, Louvre and Folies-Bergère specimens, including the four Loïe Fuller, &c, are shown. A complete set of the Grasset posters; the whole of the Toulouse-Lautrec series, the Steinlen posters, the principal works of Ibels and Bonnard, Forain, Choubrac, Grevin, Metivet, Mayet, Amand, Jean and a numerous selection of Willette, form the leading features of the French school. The English posters by Herkomer, Fowler, Walter Crane, Schmalz, Sumner, Steer, Dudley Hardy, Aubrey Beardsley, and the notorious Oxford burlesque of the latter's Avenue Theatre production; and these of Mempes, Greiffenhagen, Cleaver, Morrow and others are already known.*

The posters were displayed on an upper gallery called the 'promenade' (INSIDE COVER). There was a similar 'promenade' at the Empire Theatre, which was nearly shut down at the very same time on account of alleged soliciting taking place. Similarly, the Aquarium was felt to be dubious, as is attested by a letter of complaint in the London Metropolitan Archives. Some contemporary reviews mention the suitability of the Aquarium as a place of entertainment for showing the posters, since one could glance down from the exhibition on the promenade to the floor show below.

The numerous reviews of the exhibition discuss it in terms similar to those we would use today. Chéret, the father of the poster, is singled out, both by number of exhibits and by seniority, by almost every reviewer. Their comments remain apposite over a century later:

In delicacy of touch and strength of colour nothing can compare with the daring productions of Chéret, which bring back so many reminiscences of Paris. Chéret appears, however, to have created a Paris of his own – a shade naughtier, and more alluring, than the city of pleasure actually is. Its various charms he freely illustrates in rather imaginative vein, for no-one supposes that such diaphanously-clad damsels as Chéret's are to be seen upon the boulevards, or that a rainbow is generally considered sufficient costume in Paris for a young person whose business in life is to publish the merits of a new pastille, lampshade or pill.

***The Daily Telegraph*, 24 October, 1894**

You may easily imagine yourself in gay Paris when face to face with some of these effective pictorial posters... At the head of the French artists stands M. Jules Chéret, a man of original and creative genius. He began as a lithographer, illuminating fashion plates and title pages of pieces of music, and has gradually climbed till he is now known as the author of some four hundred pictorial posters of notable artistic merit. Capable of designing directly upon the stone, he is capable of obtaining a delicacy of colour and freshness of line rarely equalled. No.45, representing the 'corps de ballet' in the 'Coulisses de l'Opéra', shows this in all its glory of exquisite colouring. No.51, by the same artist, 'La Loïe Fuller', is most vigorous in drawing, and exhibits in four separate prints what startling effects can be produced by simply changing the colours on the dress.

***Penny Illustrated Paper*, 10 November, 1894**

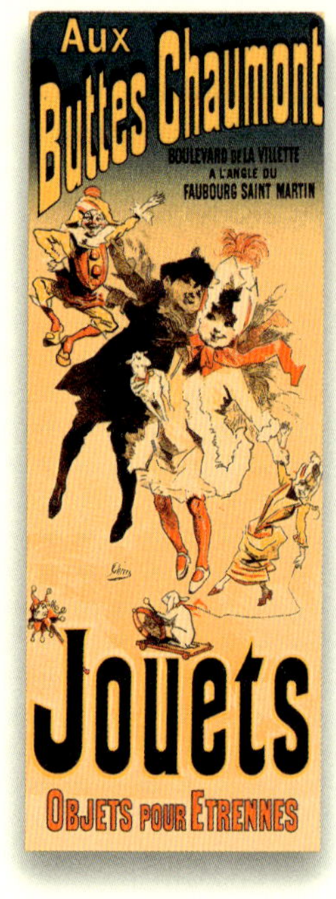

Plate 19
(above & detail, right)
Jules Chéret
(1836–1932)
Aux Buttes Chaumont: Jouets
1889
COLOUR LITHOGRAPH, 116 X 97.5 CM
Bridgeman Art Library
Private Collection
An example was shown at the London poster exhibition 1894–5, No. 24 (no price given). This image is taken from an example reproduced in Les Maîtres de l'Affiche.

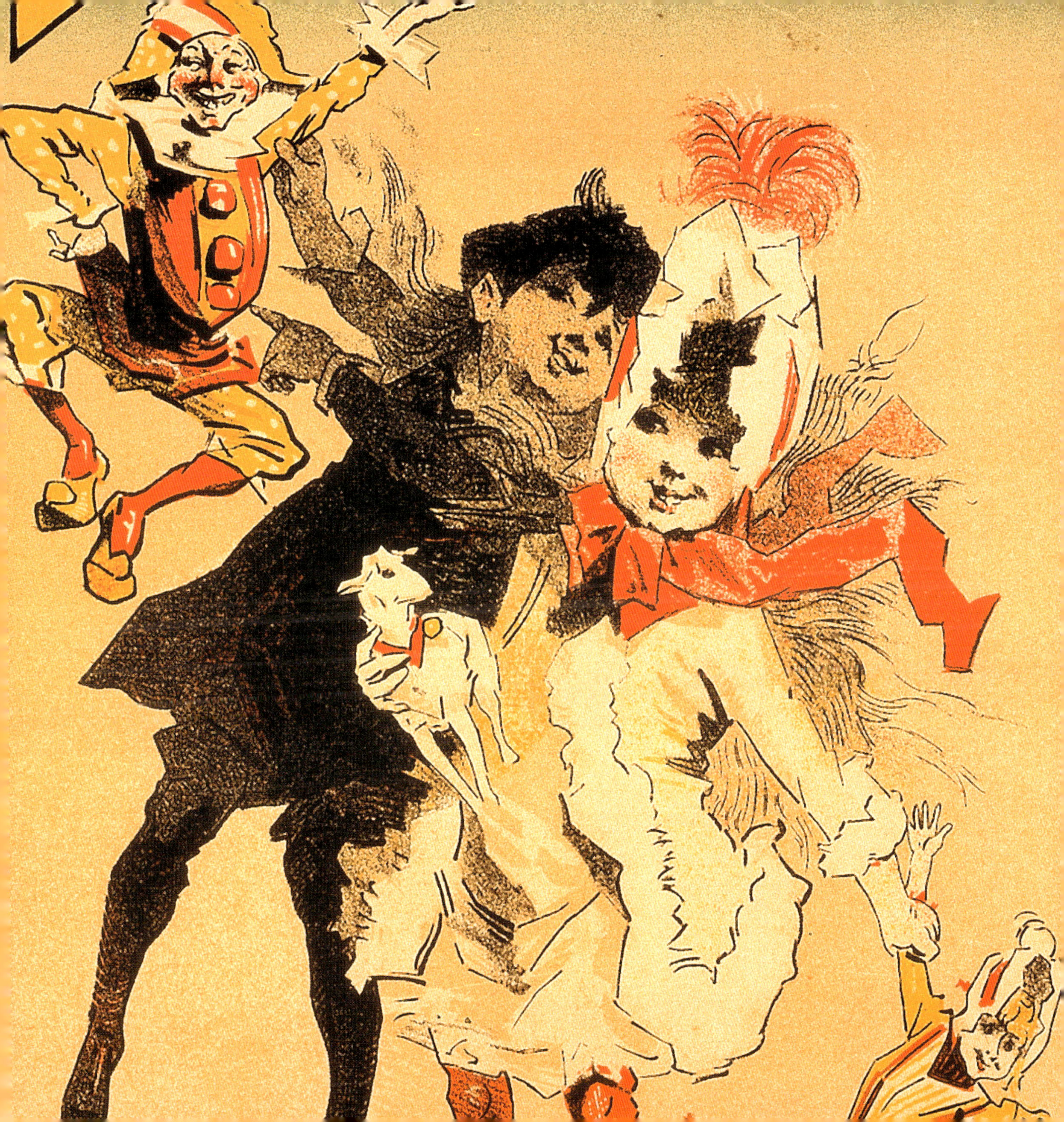

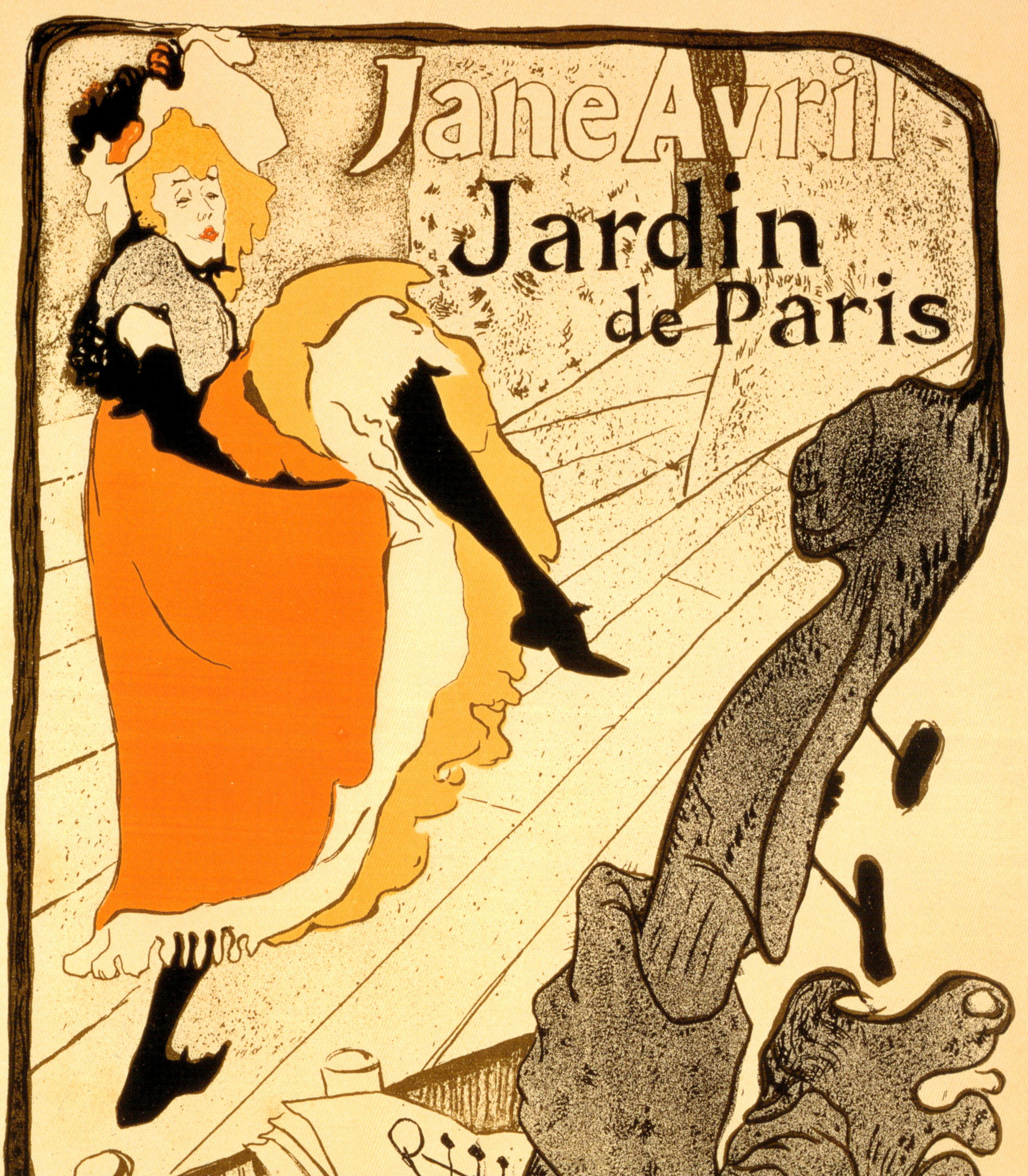
Jane Avril
Jardin
de Paris

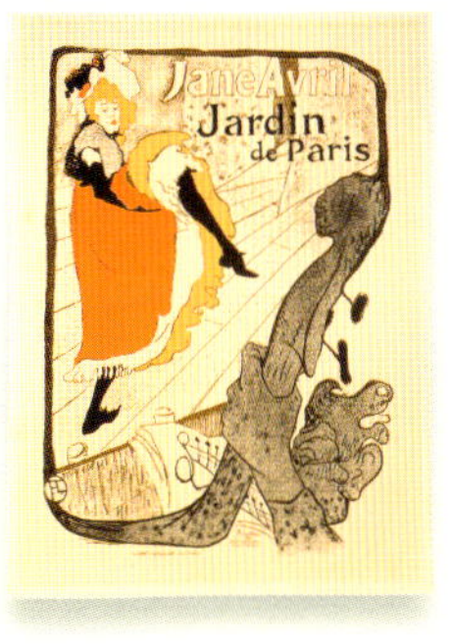

Plate 20
(above & detail, left)
Henri
de Toulouse-Lautrec
(1864–1901)
Jane Avril
1893
Colour lithograph
125 x 90 cm
Bridgeman Art Library
Private Collection
An example was shown at the London poster exhibition 1894–95. No. 127 (16/- or 80p). This image is taken from an example reproduced in Les Maîtres de l'Affiche.

Chéret is thus presented as the father of the 'artistic poster', a man of superb lithographic gifts, but he was not above using them to present a picture, both of Paris and the product he was advertising, somewhat more enticing than it really was. Naturally, his gifts were perhaps most appropriate to theatre, and theatrical subjects, where the sense of everyday reality is suspended anyway.

However, if Chéret was seen as the master, Henri de Toulouse-Lautrec was seen as the rising star. The lead here was taken by Clarke himself, in his preface in which he notes that *Among the younger men, de Toulouse-Lautrec stands pre-eminent for tremendous force, and one might almost say ruthlessness of characterization. His Jewish baron, described in the novel Reine de Joie (No.126) is an astonishing creation, which, as a type of senile lechery, deserves to be bracketed with the characters of Lionardo's* [sic] *sketchbook. Of like excellence, the café chantant singer Caudieux (No.125) seems actually to live and breathe, as he strides across his stage.*

Lautrec is generally singled out by the more specialist reviewers. The highest praise came in a magazine called *Pick-Me-Up*, whose October issue showed two cartoons directly influenced by the exhibition. In it was a review by one of the committee, the illustrator Leonard Raven-Hill (1867–1942), who singled out Lautrec and illustrated three posters by him:

Nos. 1 [*Caudieux*], 3 [*German Babylon*], 4 [*Jane Avril*] (plate 20) *are by Toulouse-Lautrec, who may be considered the most striking exponent of this branch of art. Small in actual size compared with most English posters, they simply swamp everything in their vicinity by their power of 'eye'. The average advertising agent may perhaps say they are only extraordinary, but I fancy the public will perceive other qualities in them. Look at the poster of Caudieux* (plate 4), *the 'Lion Comique', it is simply a masterpiece of effective art; think of this in comparison with the enormous head mechanically reproduced from a photograph placed on the body of a badly drawn midget, that usually serves our comedians whenever they seek pictorial advertisement. Steinlen has also done magnificent work in this line, witness his 'Yvette Guilbert' (5); how lacking in distinction most of our theatrical posters seem by its side!*

***Pick-Me-Up*, 10 November, 1894**

Other reviewers followed this lead:

Lautrec I take to be the greatest artist of them all. He affects quieter colours than his fellows: black, olive, brown, scarlet, lemon and orange. His effects are obtained with a minimum of labour, masses of ungraduated colour , and the fewest possible strong lines. His faces are full of character, and when he desires, are terribly grim or comic. Probably the best poster, taking all the requirements into consideration, shown is his 'Bruant at his Inn' , the head and shoulders of a sardonic-visaged man in profile, who wears a huge slouch hat, which is one piece of black, an Inverness cape, which is another, and a red wrapper round the throat, the end of which is tossed back over the shoulders. Seen across the width of the Aquarium this dominates everything shown; and the powerful face grips the spectator more as he draws nearer and studies it. Close

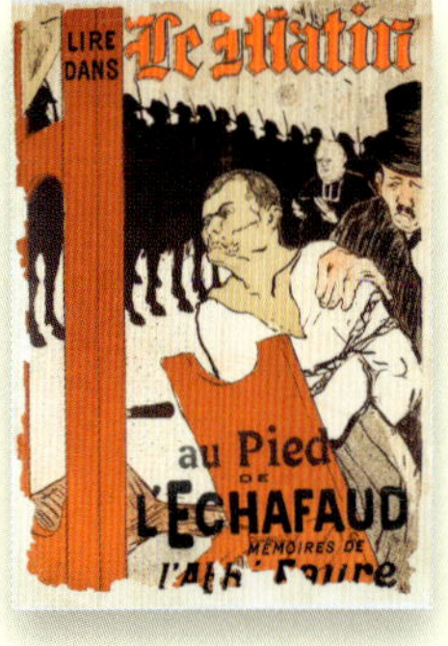

Plate 21
(above & detail, right)
Henri
de Toulouse-Lautrec
(1864–1901)
Le Matin
1893
COLOUR LITHOGRAPH
83 x 58.5 CM
V&A Images/Victoria & Albert Museum
An example was shown at the London poster exhibition 1894–5, No. 124 (12/- or 60p).

by is his poster of 'Le Matin' (PLATE 21)*, a criminal brought bound to the scaffold, his face tinted pale green, the most terribly dramatic piece of symbolic colour you can conceive; and behind, on the white ground, are tall, helmeted, cloaked and mounted soldiers in black silhouette. No need to ask the man in the street to stop and look at this.*

***Black and White,* 10 November, 1894**

This enthusiasm was echoed by the *The Daily Telegraph*:

Lautrec, on the other hand, presents us with extremely forceful posters, which almost palpitate with life. Great creative genius distinguishes them and they fulfil the aim of the poster in first attracting and then riveting the attention by their fascinating power of characterization. His portrait of Caudieux, the café-chantant singer, is an example of his best style. It possesses breadth and simplicity, which in some respects point to a careful and diligent study of Japanese art.

***The Daily Telegraph,* 24 October 1894**

Lautrec is thus presented as a slightly sinister or demonic figure, whose gifts of portrayal verge on the caricature, but with his own character and spirit. Even the *Stirling Journal*, amid derogatory comments on the British contribution, commented that the *Reine de Joie* 'has a force almost brutal in its intensity, and is indeed, perhaps strong meat for British digestion, perfected and improved as it is by the modern crusade of purity'.

On the whole the other artists were perhaps more easy to digest, since their strong decorative qualities were self-evident and did not need any warnings about the dangers of French morality to be appreciated by the British public. Steinlen was particularly appreciated, and was often seen to be the leader of the new generation:

In France it is chiefly within the last decade that artists have been giving their attention to the designing of posters. Chéret here only too fully represented, was, however, really the first to inaugurate the new movement. Whoever has been to Paris knows what gaiety and grace he has lent to the Boulevard Kiosk and the chance hoarding... but the men who have come after him have still further perfected the art. Steinlen and Guillaume, Ibels and Vallotton, have used simpler means which have proved for more telling. The silhouette is now found to be the most effective for both artistic and commercial

Plate 22
(bottom left)
Card of complaint against the Royal Aquarium, inscribed
I recommend to your observation the collection of indecent French posters on view at the Aquarium. Much worse than the Zaeo poster.
1894
London Metropolitan Archives (LCC/MIN/10,891)

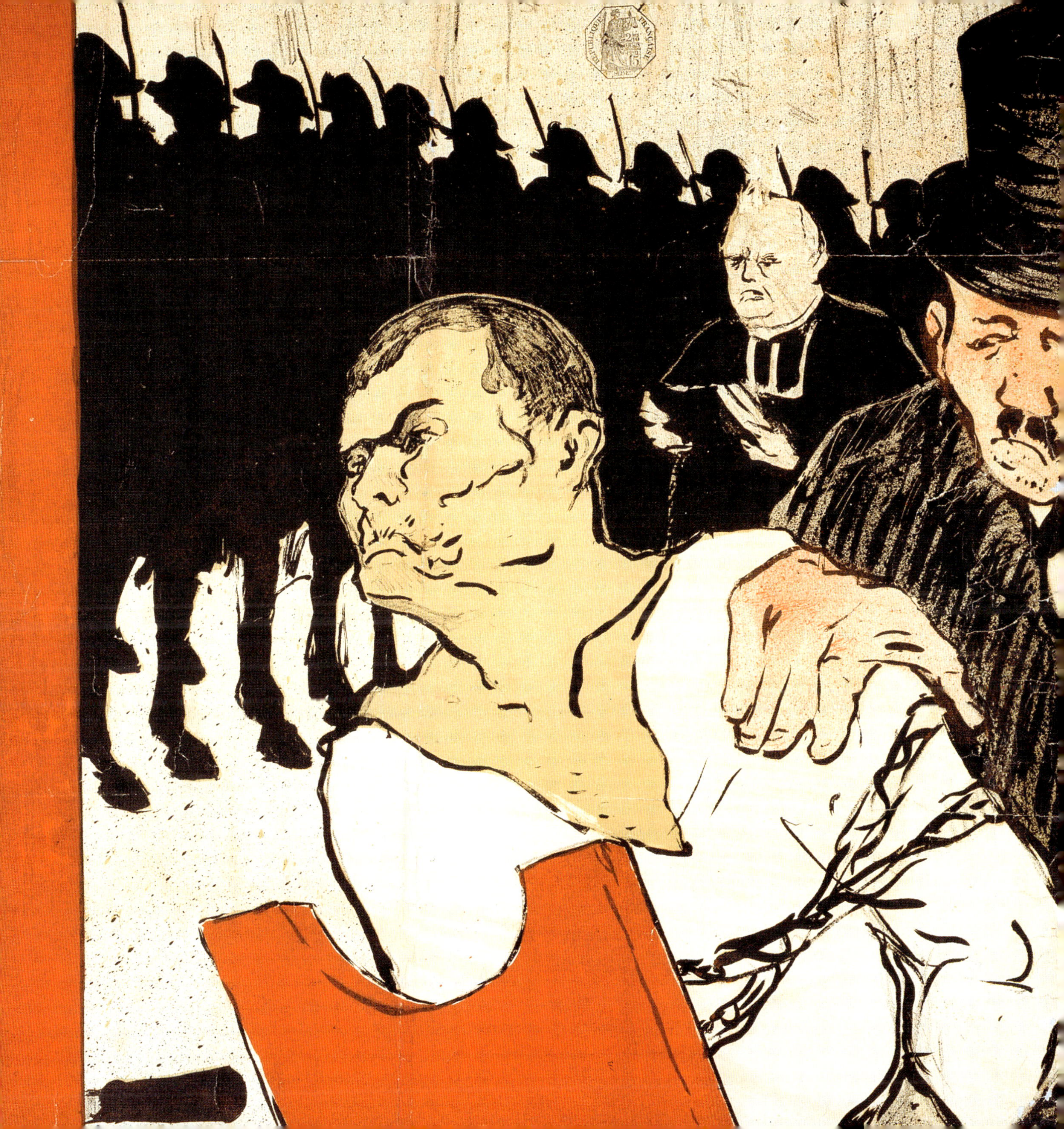
REPUBLIQUE FRANÇAISE

ends, and no artists have turned it to finer account than Lautrec and Gausson. Go and look at their work if you would understand the full measure of their triumph.

***Woman*, 31 October 1894 (signed P. E. R.)**

Only a handful of reviews claim to see any immorality or sexual impropriety in the posters of the exhibition. This is despite the racy nature of many of the posters. But at least one visitor was offended and felt compelled to write and complain and his card survives in the volume in the London Metropolitan Archives: *I recommend to/your observation/the collection of/indecent French/posters on view at the/Aquarium. Much worse than the Zaeo poster.* Unfortunately it arrived just after a committee meeting, and so was not discussed. (PLATE 22)

The reviews were so uniformly positive that a second exhibition seems to have been immediately contemplated. This exhibition, which opened on 20 March 1896, included not only French and British posters, but also Italian, Spanish and those of other countries. The up and coming name was now Alphonse Mucha, whose first poster, *Gismonda*, had been a success in 1894–5. There was also a large American contingent, featuring the work of Penfield, Bradley and others. Again, an extensively illustrated catalogue was produced. The preface was now written by Hartrick, who notes that the exhibition denoted the *triumph of the silhouette* and that Chéret *still holds the first place in France in his own line, though run somewhat close by Meunier, while Lautrec, toning down somewhat his more outré and grotesque method, has given us two very charming portraits of ladies.* Most interestingly, there was a design by Lautrec for the poster *Whisky*, which Hartrick later claimed in his autobiography was a favourite tipple of Lautrec.[8] Most of the exhibits of the 1896 exhibition were lent by Bella, and only a few have come to the Victoria and Albert Museum by occasional later purchase or gift.

Lautrec must have been thoroughly heartened by the reception of his work in the two exhibitions. He had also featured strongly in Charles Hiatt's book *Picture Posters*, London, 1895, which included his unpublished design of Yvette Guilbert as frontispiece, owing to Lautrec's kindness. In *The Magazine of Art* for 1896–7, a review of lithography by H. M. Spielmann notes that *lastly, amongst the leaders (in France) must be accounted M. Toulouse-Lautrec. For him the stone does not count for very much, but with the pencil he wields with so much facility and power of reproducing concentrated character he seeks to prove himself descendant of Gavarni and Daumier.* Specimens of his work were shown, with other French works, at two meetings at the Royal Society of Arts in 1896 and 1897. The first meeting was chaired by one of the 1894 exhibition committee members, Ernest Hart, who had earlier (1894) contributed articles on Japanese art. He and Edward Bella lent a variety of posters for this meeting, including Lautrec's *Bruant*, *Confetti* and *Caudieux*. Here the Chairman of the Art Workers' Guild Lewis F. Day (1845–1910) spoke of Chéret's 'objectionable Frenchiness' but recognized his skills as a lithographer. The artist Joseph Pennell (1860–1926) said that Chéret *had gone on turning the handle of the organ that he had been turning for years; it was always the same female figure, standing on one or other leg, or holding a flag or something else in the other hand, and he did not think there was any advance in his work at all... Lautrec and Ibels were fine, but they are fine draughtsmen.*

Reviews such as these must have given Lautrec the confidence to attempt a one-man show at the Goupil Gallery in London in 1898, which was not a success. He died in 1901, without apparently trying to sell any more of his work in England. When, twenty years later, the widow of Joseph Thacher Clarke offered her husband's collection of posters to the Victoria and Albert Museum, she stated that they had come from the first exhibition of posters held in London. She asked only a nominal sum for the posters by Chéret, who was

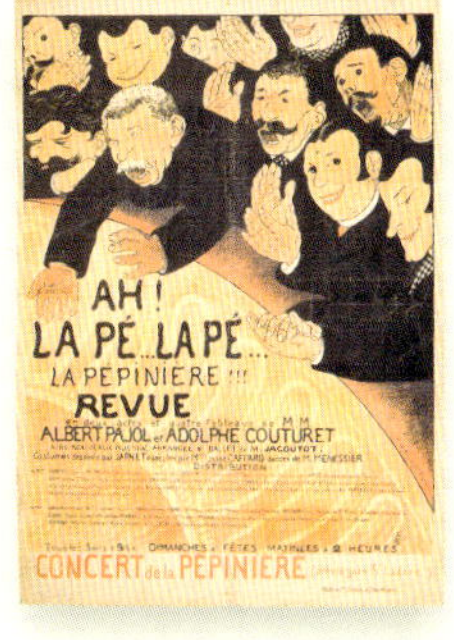

Plate 23
(above & detail, right)
Félix Vallotton
(1865 – 1925)
Ah! La Pé... La Pé...
La Pépinière
Colour lithograph
122 x 90 cm
V&A Images/Victoria & Albert Museum
An example was shown at the London poster exhibition 1894–5, No. 178 (6/- or 30p)

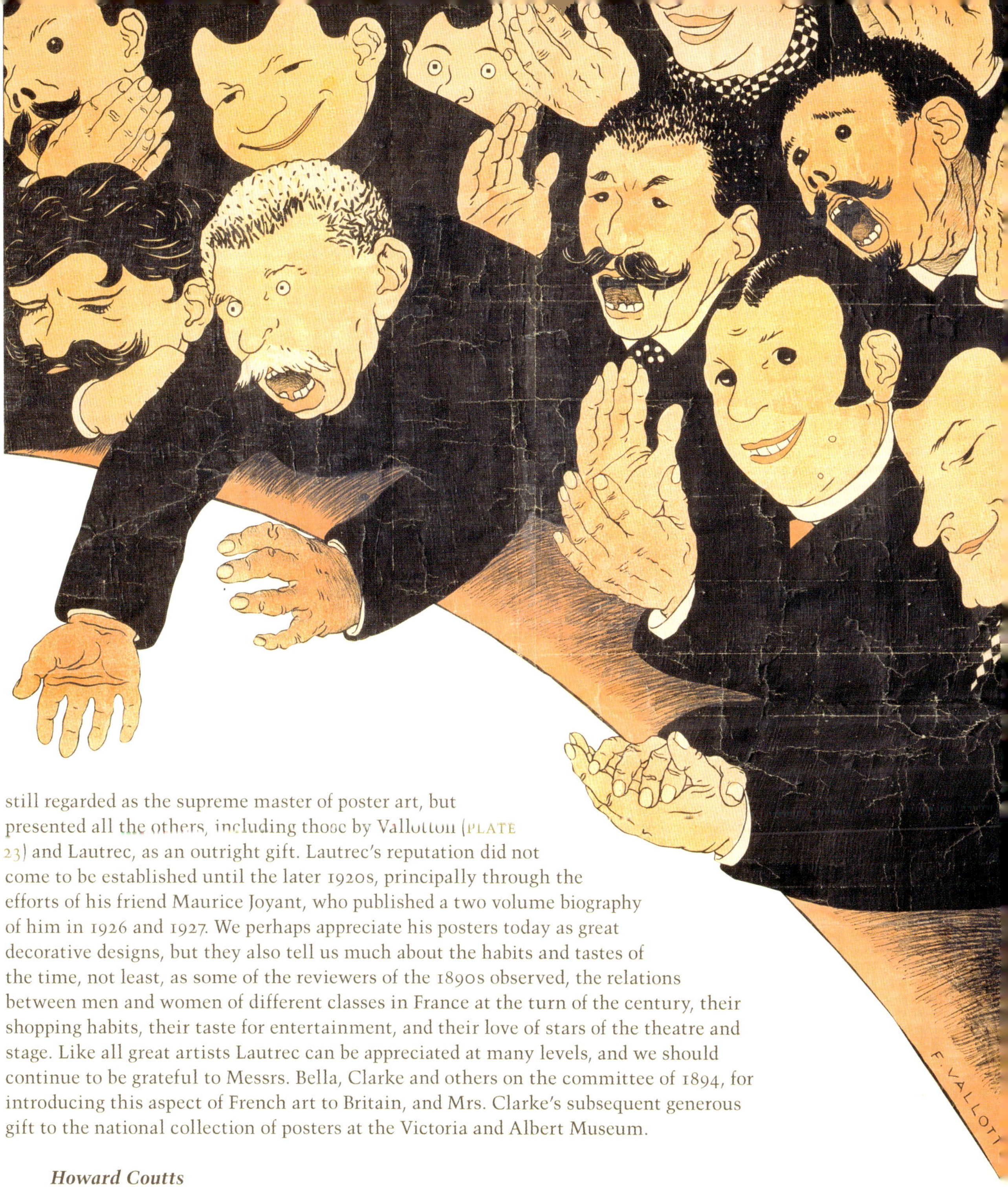

still regarded as the supreme master of poster art, but presented all the others, including those by Vallotton (plate 23) and Lautrec, as an outright gift. Lautrec's reputation did not come to be established until the later 1920s, principally through the efforts of his friend Maurice Joyant, who published a two volume biography of him in 1926 and 1927. We perhaps appreciate his posters today as great decorative designs, but they also tell us much about the habits and tastes of the time, not least, as some of the reviewers of the 1890s observed, the relations between men and women of different classes in France at the turn of the century, their shopping habits, their taste for entertainment, and their love of stars of the theatre and stage. Like all great artists Lautrec can be appreciated at many levels, and we should continue to be grateful to Messrs. Bella, Clarke and others on the committee of 1894, for introducing this aspect of French art to Britain, and Mrs. Clarke's subsequent generous gift to the national collection of posters at the Victoria and Albert Museum.

Howard Coutts

Impressions of late-nineteenth century Paris

Paris of the Belle Époque

THE LAST DECADE of the French nineteenth century is commonly known as the *'Belle Époque'* or the 'beautiful age'.[9] France was full of optimism. In 1889 it had witnessed the opening of the Eiffel Tower and of the cabaret, the *Moulin Rouge*, and in 1900 the International Exhibition, lit by electricity, drew thousands of visitors to Paris. As the economy flourished, the burgeoning middle class sought diversion and entertainment from their working lives. Promoters and entrepreneurs, keen to foster the mood of this modern time, avidly embraced the poster to market their products. Posters both responded to and created new desires as diverse as bicycles, entertainment venues and the latest and most fashionable in interior decoration (PLATE 24).

A new Paris was being created, one of order and confidence, which proclaimed Paris as a world cultural and technological leader. The projects begun under Napoleon III's Second Empire (1852–1870) by the city planner Baron Haussmann, and new initiatives such as the Paris metro, continued to transform Paris well into the twentieth century. Working class tenements were pulled down and replaced with wide, paved, tree-lined boulevards which crossed the city in strategic lines, allowing greater movement of goods and people than ever before.

The new department stores began to congregate along the boulevards, creating monumental cathedrals to consumerism. In 1883, the French author, Émile Zola, proclaimed:

... the department store tends to replace the church. It marches to the religion of the cash desk, of coquetry, and fashion, [women] *go there to pass the hours as they used to go to church: an occupation, a place of enthusiasm where they struggle between their passion for clothes and the thrift of their husbands...*[10]

The crowd, constantly distracted by new products and diversions, replaced the concept of the mob, which had repeatedly threatened Paris' stability over the previous decades, most recently during the Paris Commune of 1871. Through the development of the department store, improved transport, economic prosperity and the rise of the middle class, new commodities and markets emerged which constantly vied with each other for attention. The poster developed to become the intermediary between consumer and retailer.

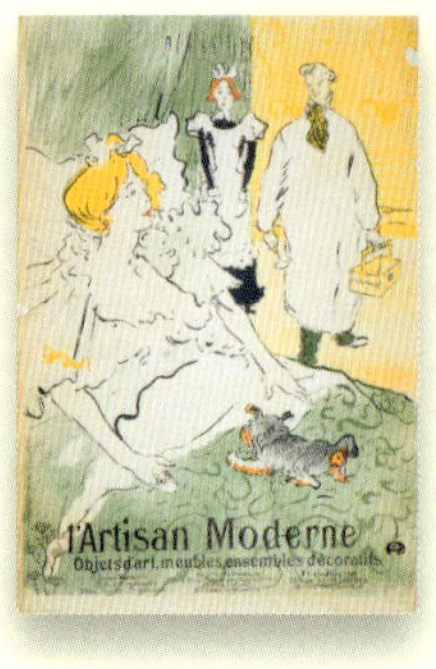

Plate 24
(above & detail, right)
Henri
de Toulouse-Lautrec
(1864–1901)
L'Artisan Moderne
1894
COLOUR LITHOGRAPH
93.5 X 65 CM
V&A Images/Victoria & Albert Museum

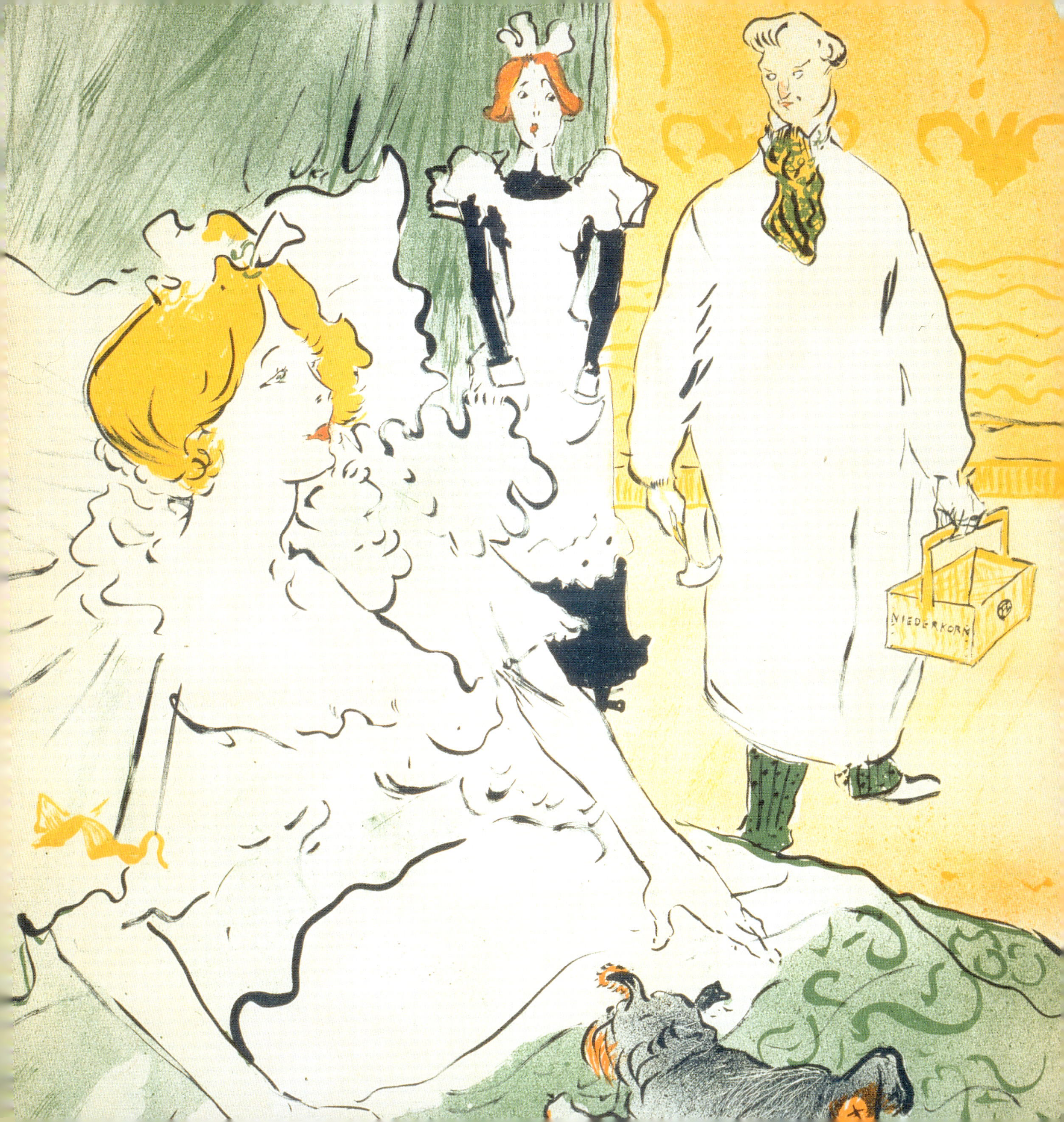
NIEDERKORN

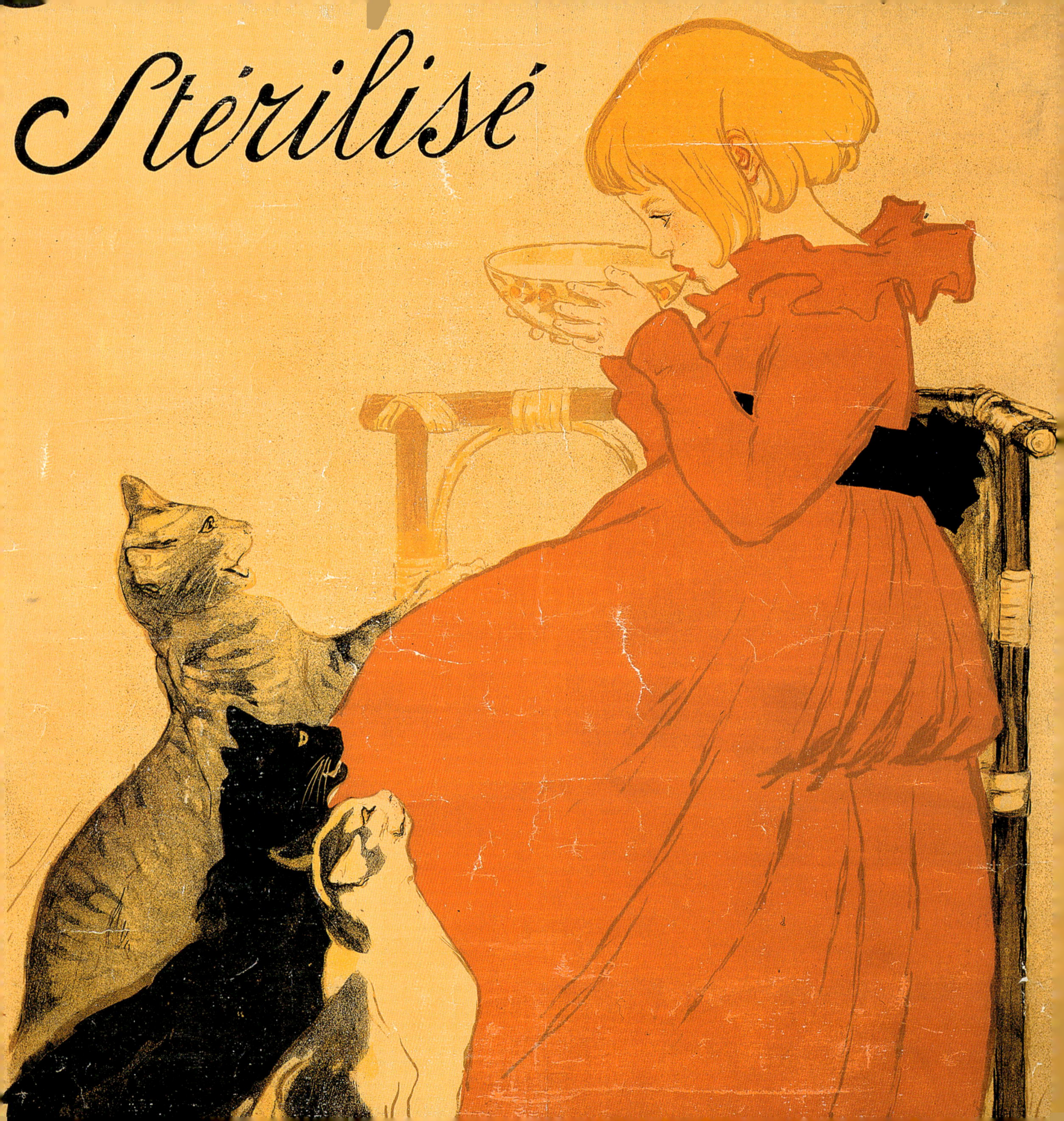
Stérilisé

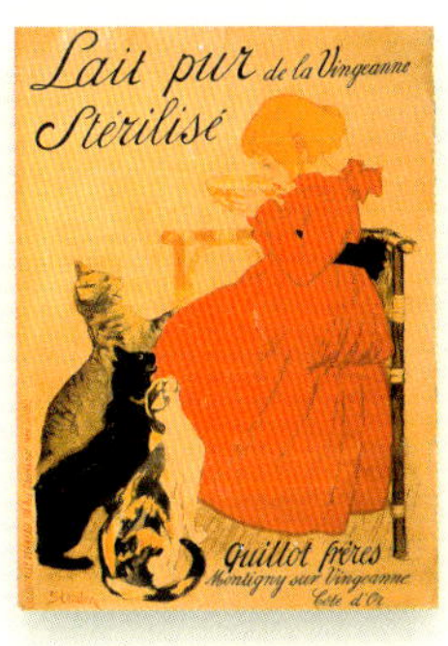

Plate 25
(above & detail, left)
Théophile-Alexandre Steinlen
(1859–1923)
Lait Pur Stérilisé
1894
Colour lithograph
133 x 99 cm
V&A Images/Victoria & Albert Museum
An example was shown at the London poster exhibition 1894–5, No. 175 (6/ or 30p)

The exhibition, *Toulouse-Lautrec and the Art of the French Poster*, recreates parts of the poster exhibitions held in London in 1894–5 and 1896. The posters are indicative of an era, of its needs and desires. They vividly depict toiletries and cosmetics, from toothpaste to face creams; entertainment venues such as the Moulin Rouge and the Chat Noir; new plays, shows, and magazines; coffee, hot chocolate, and sterilised milk. Posters advertising bicycles and train journeys emphasised new freedoms brought on by industrialisation and a buoyant economy. These posters all once rubbed shoulders on the streets of Paris, vying for attention with those promoting the cabaret and theatre stars of the day, like Sarah Bernhardt, Jane Avril and Aristide Bruant.

Representing social 'types' through posters

The posters in this exhibition are indicative of this new, affluent and confident Paris, and of contemporary preoccupations with health, entertainment, and progress. They nearly all feature easily identifiable social 'types' such as the contented child, the aristocrat, glamorous women, and the cabaret stars of the day. These types imbue each product with a specific quality that appeals to a given aspiration, such as improved health or the desire to escape from daily life by being entertained. As Williamson observes in *Decoding Advertisements*, advertisements have to make the product mean something to us, [they] *are selling us something besides consumer goods… they are selling us ourselves.*[11]

In 1894 the Swiss artist T. A. Steinlen (1859–1923) was commissioned to create an image for the Quillot brothers' dairy. The result is the poster, *Lait Pur Stérilisé* [Pure Sterilised Milk] which depicts a well-fed middle class child drinking milk surrounded by her jealous pet cats (plate 25). This was Steinlen's first poster, and yet it has become one of the all-time most endearing poster images ever created. The model is Steinlen's own daughter, Colette.

In this poster, a healthy child 'type' is used to promote a modern hygiene product. The young girl presents an idealised image of childhood. Childhood itself was a relatively new concept, developed in particular by the French philosopher Jean Jacques Rousseau (1712–78) who believed in the importance of child education as a means to improving society. By the 1890s the regeneration of Paris (at least for the middle class), new sewerage systems, child labour laws, and a lower birth rate, improved conditions for children and furthered our modern conceptions of childhood. There continued to be concerns over prostitution, child labour, and poverty.[12] According to Weisberg:

… with the rise of the bourgeoisie and their disposable income, the child no longer needed to work… [but] *became a priceless jewel at the centre of a family's reason for existence…. This reverence for the innocent, indulged child became widely apparent* [in the late nineteenth century], *serving as a counterpoint to the urban beggar who wandered the streets in search of food or a sou.*[13]

It is not hard to imagine this large, brightly coloured poster pasted on a Paris street, beneath which child workers, beggars and prostitutes passed on their daily grind.

Indeed, the healthy, playful child 'type' also reveals something of society's fears. Cholera epidemics were still a threat, although Haussmann's introduction of a new and extensive sewerage system largely ended the outbreaks of cholera which had regularly decimated the population, taking more than 16,000 lives in Paris in 1849. In 1893, Louis Pasteur isolated the microbe. Poster artists exploited this invisible threat, either directly or indirectly, to sell products (particularly aimed at middle class mothers) that alleged to protect the family's health. Healthy child types were used to sell new foodstuffs such as sterilised milk and packaged biscuits that represented the latest in the fight against disorder and disease.

Boutet de Monvel (1851–1913) was a French painter and watercolourist who created only a few posters in his lifetime. His experience in illustrating children's literature and his modern style, combined to create striking posters such as that for *Pâte Dentifrice du Docteur Pierre* (Doctor Pierre's toothpaste) (PLATE 26). It depicts a young, composed girl, in a private bathroom hung with a contemporary wall paper, wearing modern dress. The strap line assures the public that the toothpaste is 'en vente partout', on sale everywhere, indicating that this picture of health, hygiene and progress, is available to all by purchasing this particular brand of toothpaste.

In contrast, de Monvel's poster for the operetta *La Petite Poucette* (Little Miss Hop-o'-My-Thumb) presents a young girl braving the elements with a large red umbrella which forms the centrepiece to the poster. Her costume is provincial and working class, and suggests a tale of hardship and aspirations.

Posters also make use of children to advertise department stores, particularly in the run up to Christmas. The commercialisation of Christmas grew throughout the late nineteenth century, pushed by the new department stores, who turned new aspirations of childhood to their advantage. Jules Chéret (1836–1932) created various designs for Paris department stores. His colourful, dynamic style was a perfect medium to attract customers to the delights of this modern consumer paradise. Choice and leisure are themes evident in his posters, as well as the importance of children's games. Since Rousseau, play had been championed as an intrinsic part of child development. The concept of childhood as a liberated, playful period in a person's life, devoid of the struggles and hardships of adult life, are evident in Chéret's posters for the department stores Aux Buttes Chaumont (PLATE 19) and Grands Magasins du Louvre. The children in his posters tumble and cascade, overjoyed with the toys and gifts they have received.

If images of children can be seen to embody a new interest in childhood, images of women tend to affirm them either as embodiments of domesticity or as diversions from that very domesticity. Chéret's series of posters for the Saxoléine company present vivacious fashionable women holding lamps fuelled by the company's *'pétrôle de sureté'*, dependable paraffin oil (PLATE 18).

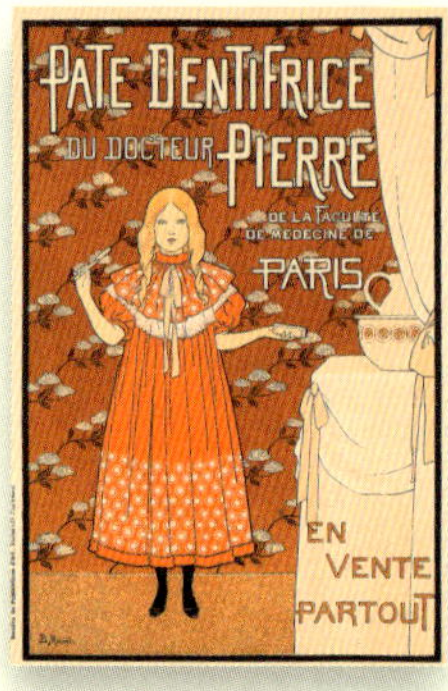

Plate 26
(above & detail, right)
Louis Maurice Boutet de Monvel
(1851–1913)
Pâte Dentifrice du Docteur Pierre
1894
COLOUR LITHOGRAPH
82 X 61 CM
Bridgeman Art Library
Private Collection
An example was shown at the London poster exhibition 1894–5, No. 15 (4/- or 20p). This image is from an example reproduced in Les Maîtres de l'Affiche.

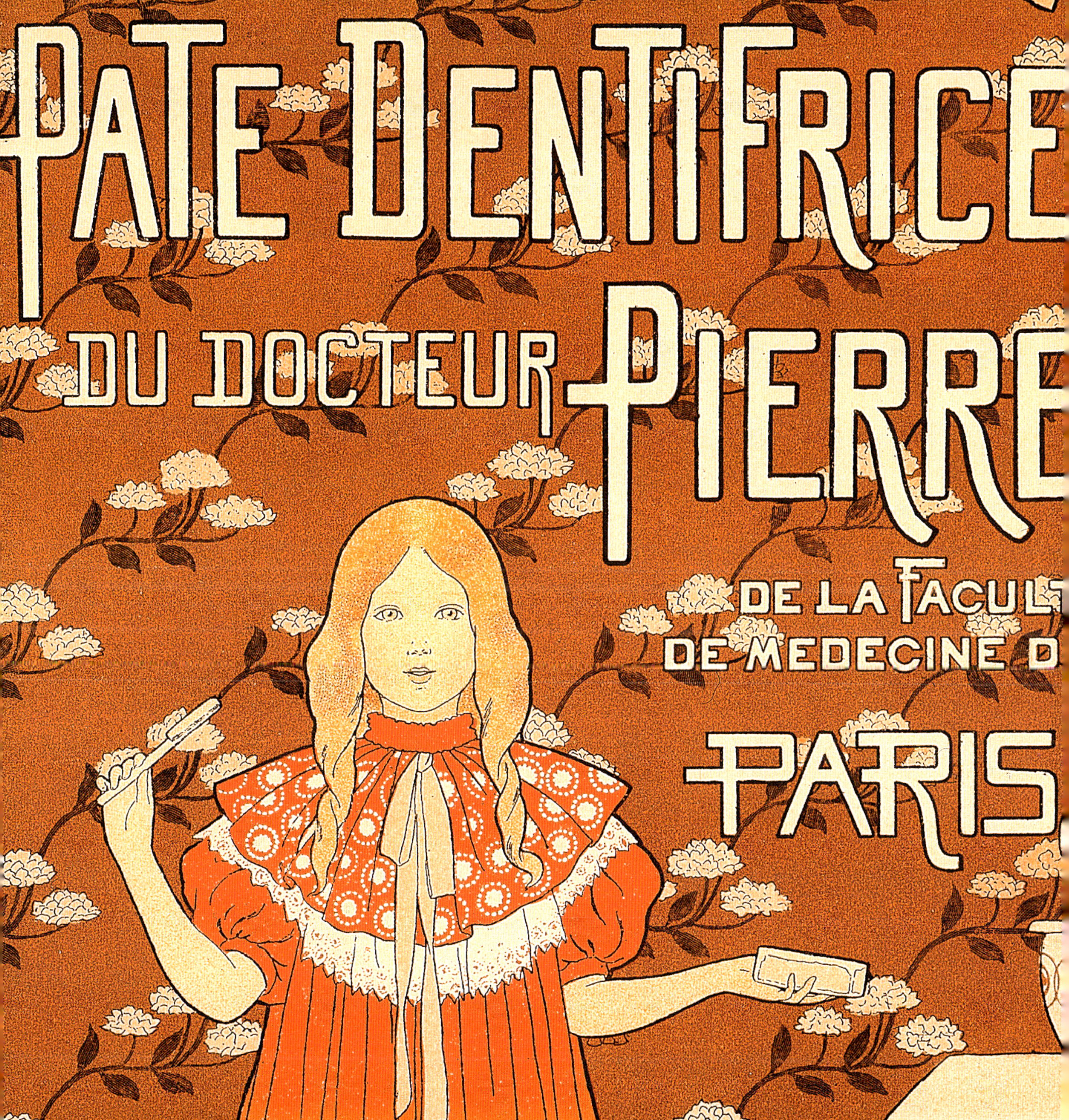
PATE DENTIFRICE
DU DOCTEUR PIERRE
DE LA FACULT
DE MEDECINE D
PARIS

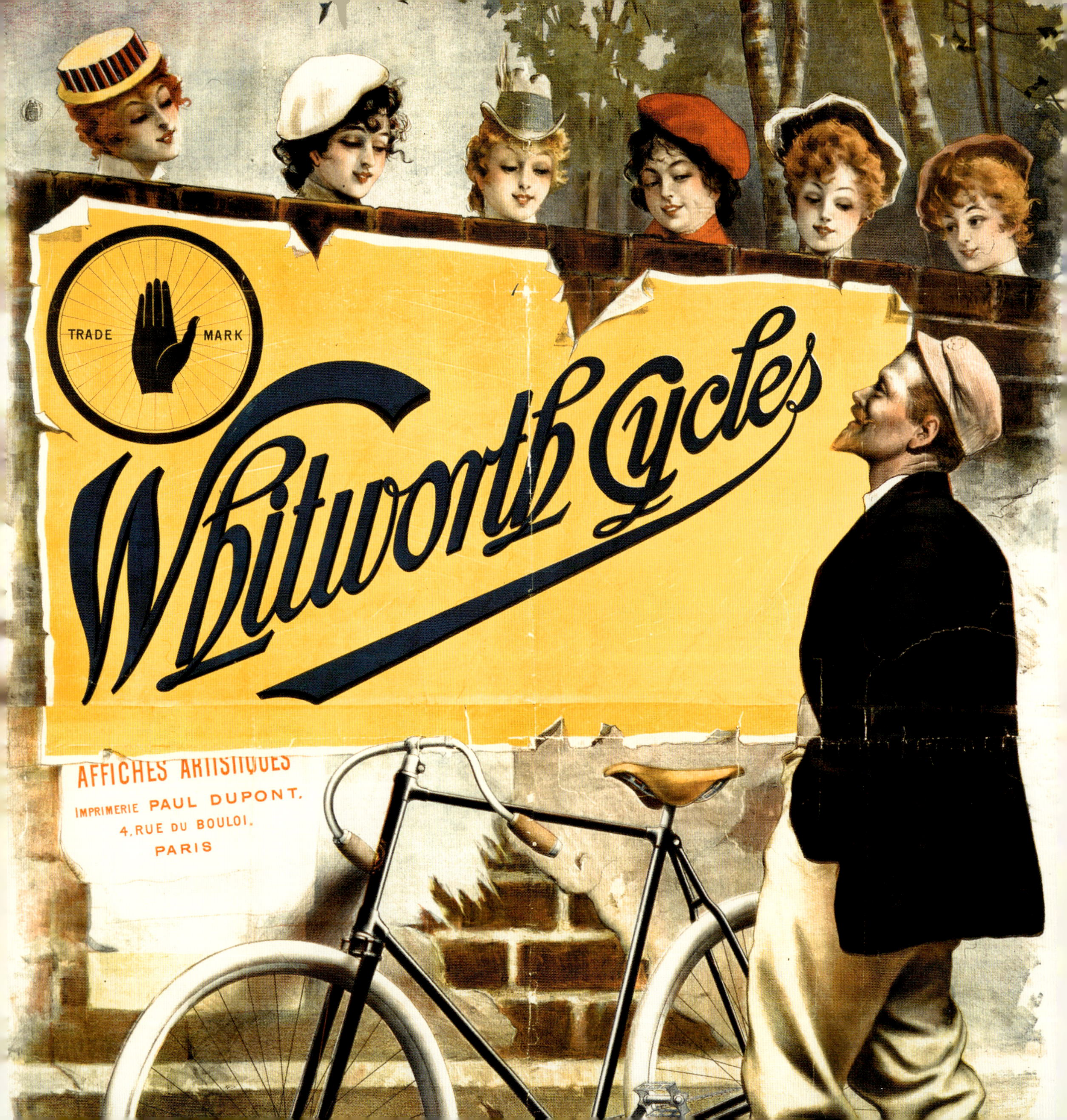
TRADE MARK
Whitworth Cycles
AFFICHES ARTISTIQUES
IMPRIMERIE PAUL DUPONT,
4, RUE DU BOULOI,
PARIS

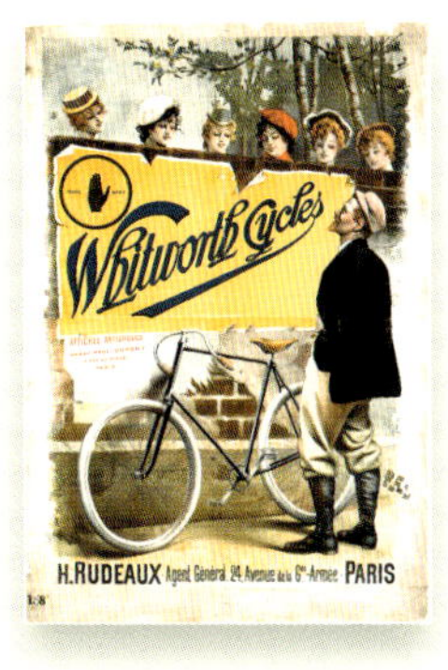

Plate 27
(above & detail, left)
Jean de Paleologue
(Pal)
(1860–1942)
Whitworth Cycles
1894
COLOUR LITHOGRAPH
220 X 138 CM
V&A Images/Victoria & Albert Museum
This example was shown at the London poster exhibition 1894–5, No. 158 (6/- or 30p) (bears original exhibition number on bottom left).

The woman in a green dress shows pleasure in the bright light produced by the oil, described as extra white, odourless and inflammable. These qualities, as well as the class of women portrayed, enforce notions of hygiene and safety combined with fashion and luxury. The woman communicates her family's social position and aspirations. Long before advertisers began to talk about product recognition, Chéret was creating it with his Saxoléine posters.[14] The product itself, a bottle of paraffin, is not shown.

These women and children, however, are generally treated as solitary creatures. An exception is *Whitworth Cycles* by Jean de Paleologue (1860–1942), also known as PAL (PLATE 27).

The bicycle was just one of the late nineteenth century developments in transport which revolutionised people's lives. In Paris, the wider roads developed by Haussmann provided new avenues for the circulation of bicycles and trams. This particular poster depicts a group of women in fashionable headgear, in conversation with a male cyclist.[15] The message is one of sociability, rather than exercise. Indeed, it suggests that this new mode of transport has the power to attract the opposite sex. Here, the poster is selling not just a product, but an image of freedom and modernity. As Goldman observes, *Things produced by human activity take on the appearance of active agents. Witness the tendency to endow certain marketed goods with the power to create a social situation like an enjoyable weekend.*[16]

Representing Paris through posters and memoirs

THE 1894–5 LONDON POSTER EXHIBITION, which this exhibition recreates in part, brought with it scenes of popular Parisian entertainment to Victorian London. These posters have left a lasting legacy that continues to inform our perception of Paris, rooted in the hedonist days of the *Belle Époque*. Montmartre in particular has been mythologised through literature, paintings, and above all, through the art of the poster. Our image of Paris is of the night, inextricably bound to these colourful, vivid and arresting images, which offered a world of freedom and entertainment. The walls of Paris exploded with dazzling images of countless, affordable spectacles, all vying to catch the eye of the passer-by.

The centre of this poster revolution was Montmartre. A hillside area to the north west of central Paris, Montmartre was notorious for its dance halls, bars and brothels, and had long been a refuge of artists, criminals and drunks. In 1860 the area was finally absorbed into the city, becoming the eighteenth arrondissement, or district. By the late nineteenth century, fuelled by economic prosperity and improved transport links, the area had become a centre of music halls, vaudeville shows, circuses and café-concerts that offered a respite from the daily grind. These included the Cirque Fernando, Aristide Bruant's cabaret Le Mirliton, Adolphe Salis' Le Chat Noir, renowned for its shadow plays and, above all, the Moulin Rouge, which opened its doors on 5 October 1889 (PLATE 28).

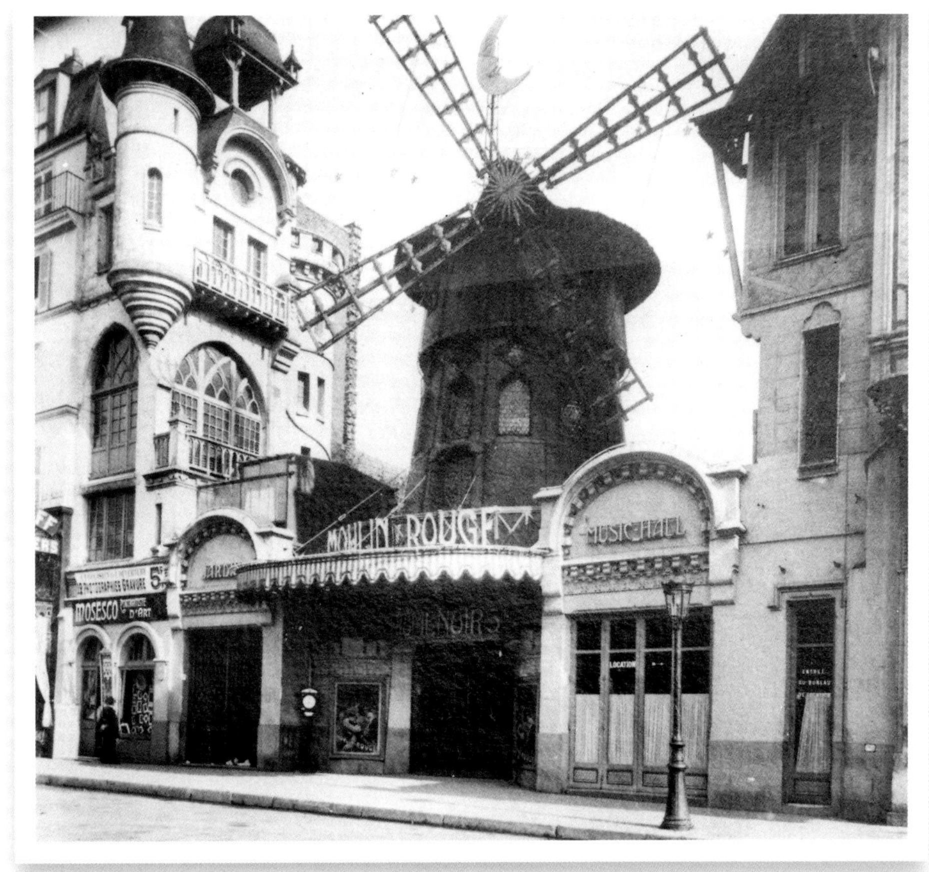

Plate 28 (left)
Eugène Atget (1856–1927)
The Moulin Rouge, Paris
1921
Black and White Photograph
Bridgeman Guiradon/ Lauros

Entrepreneurs constantly vied with each other to present the newest, and the most sophisticated entertainment, and embraced the poster as a medium to promote their venues and star attractions. According to Weisberg, *if bohemian commercialism opened the neighbourhood to a more broadly based clientele, these* bals publics *– or at least those that survived – perfected the techniques of mass publicity.*[17]

Into this world entered Henri de Toulouse-Lautrec (1864–1901), who thrived on Montmartre's nightlife and its personalities and whose paintings and posters have become synonymous with Paris, its nightlife, and the *Belle Époque*. When Lautrec moved to Montmartre in 1884 he joined other artists including Degas, Van Gogh, Seurat, Renoir, Vuillard and Bonnard. However, Lautrec did not adhere to any art movement, or indeed to any particular political party. Rather, his interest was in observing people, their personalities and social interactions.

As Lautrec himself stated, *I have tried to depict the true and not the ideal. It is a defect, perhaps, for warts do not find favour in my eyes, and I like to embellish them with playful fur, to round them, and to put a shining end on them. I do not know if you bridle your pen, but when my pencil moves, it is necessary to let it go, or – crash!... nothing more.*

Lautrec was to produce over thirty works related to Montmartre, in the form of posters, lithographs and paintings. His first poster, for the Moulin Rouge, *Le Moulin Rouge – La Goulue* is indicative of his style and approach (PLATE 13).

The poster depicts the interior of the Moulin Rouge with a pair of dancers dancing *le chahut*, the forerunner of the cancan. La Goulue, or The Glutton (1886–1929), was one of the most notorious dancers of the day, and is shown provocatively raising her petticoats. The dancer Valentin le Désossé, or Valentin the Boneless accompanies her. The audience is depicted in silhouette, reminiscent of the oriental-inspired shadow plays that had become fashionable in Paris. The sea of top hats denote affluent types, their silhouettes suggesting the anonymous freedom of the Moulin Rouge. The power of this poster was immediately recognised. Within a year it had been exhibited at three exhibitions, and been illustrated in a monograph.[18] The names of Lautrec, La Goulue, Montmartre, and the Moulin Rouge, would be indelibly linked in our perception of Paris of the *Belle Époque*.

Many of Lautrec's posters promoted contemporary cabaret stars. The singer and cabaret owner Aristide Bruant (1851–1925) quickly realised the potential not only of the poster, but Lautrec's skill as a poster artist. When he starred at the Ambassadeurs cabaret in 1892, he persuaded the venue's director to plaster the venue with the poster he had had designed by Lautrec, and to display it all over Paris (PLATE 29).[19] By so doing Bruant contributed not inconsiderably to Lautrec's fame, but also to his own, and to the mythologising of Montmartre. Bruant embodied Montmartre. His song writing blended (leftist) political ideas with working class *argot* or street language, and he delighted his audiences with his insulting treatment of them. He was popular with the aristocracy and with intellectuals, who were titillated by this sanitised political and working class rhetoric. To quote Sweetman, the success of venues such as these *was proof that you could get rich from political entertainment, provided it was just that – entertainment.*[20]

In the 1920s, prompted by rumours of the re-opening of the Moulin Rouge, an English author, Arthur Symons, wrote his memoirs, lamenting the passing of old Montmartre.[21] These essays are aimed at an English (male) audience, and both attract and repel the reader. For Symons, Montmartre, and particularly the Moulin Rouge, was synonymous with vice and licentious behaviour. His essays are peppered with references to flames, the colour red, sewers and the night. Even the streets of Paris, despite the new boulevards, and gas and electric lighting, are described as follows:

... one is plunged into a hideously heated nightmare out of which surge strange sensations, animal faces; men dressed in black, women dressed in sombre costumes,

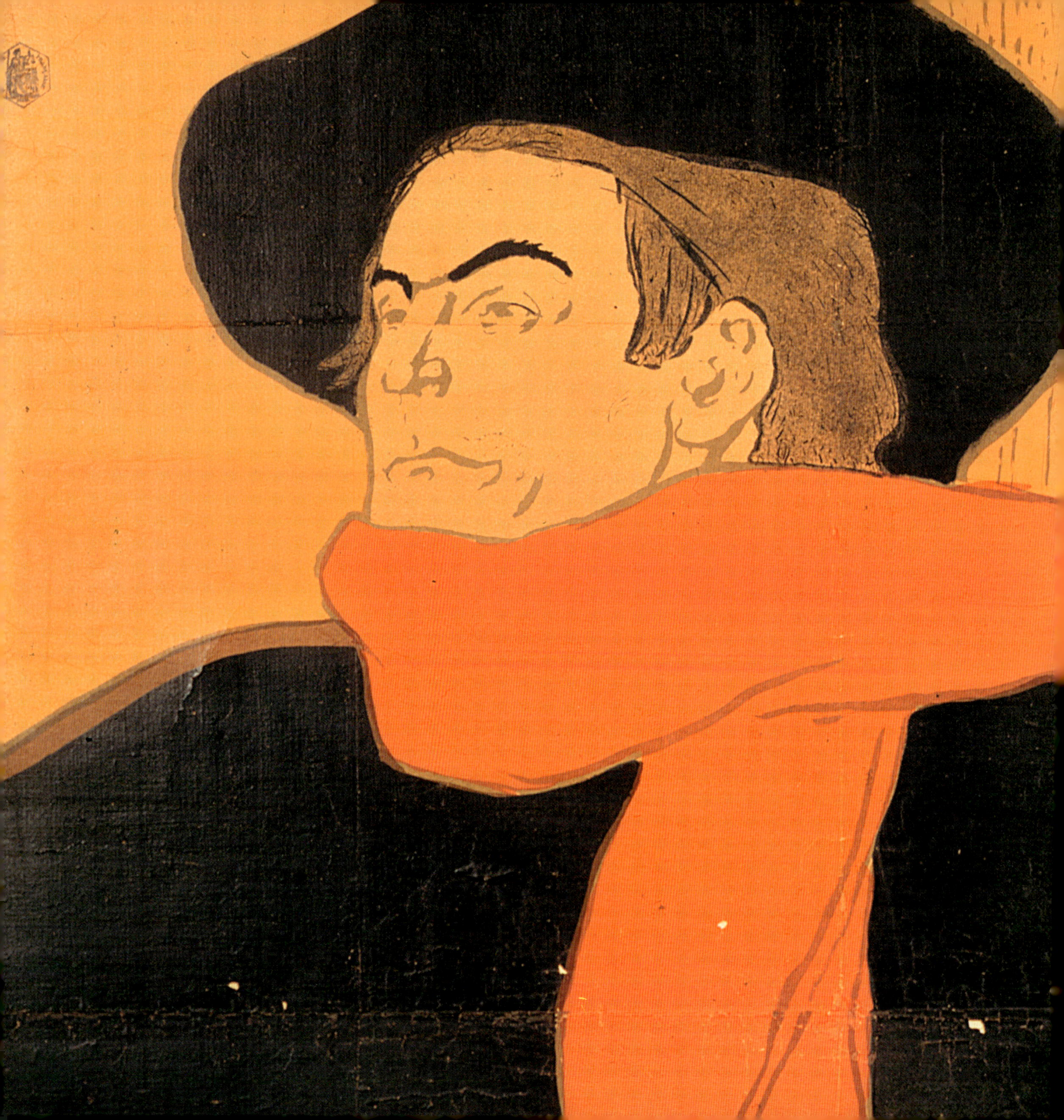

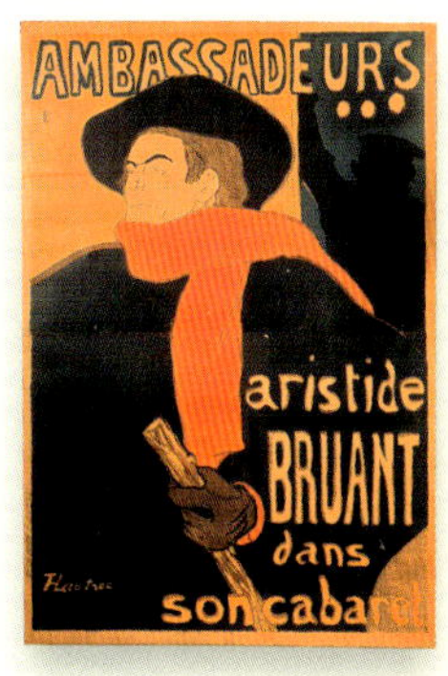

Plate 29
(above & detail, left)
Henri
de Toulouse-Lautrec
(1864–1901)
Aristide Bruant
1892
Colour lithograph
136 x 97 cm
Bridgeman Art Library
Victoria & Albert Museum
An example was shown at the London poster exhibition 1894–5, No. 121 (15/- or 75p)

who seem to be sorceresses, demons, beasts of the night such as one sees in the paintings of those who have portrayed the temptation which St. Antony endured in the seventh circle of hell.[22]

Reading Symons, you become a voyeur, stepping through a debris of humanity, guided by him through the obscurity of this world so that, from the comfort of your English home, you yourself can experience the Paris cabarets and be titillated by their licentious behaviour. Symons describes in detail his visits in 1892 to two cabarets, Le Mirliton and Le Chat Noir. Despite these venues' mass promotional techniques through the poster, they are presented as underground venues, only accessible to the initiated or the brave. For example, his description of entering Le Mirliton is as follows:

...it has the appearance of a small shop after working hours... There is no name over the door, and nothing of the interior can be seen but those few panes of coloured glass, only half covered, and behind them, at intervals, the flash of a match. Through the closed doors comes the sound of loud voices, the jingle of a piano, the words of a song... For a nervous person to visit the Mirliton is rather an ordeal. You come up to the noisy, masked and guarded place; you knock at the door that seems never made to open; and presently you hear the harsh, grating sound of two bolts being drawn back. The door does, indeed, open, but the man who opens it scrutinises you from head to foot, and, if you do not please him, he will refuse you admittance. A lady is never refused admittance, but the chances are that she pays a toll in a kiss... Inside, as you look round, you find yourself in a small room, with a yet smaller room opening out of it. It is a little in the style of a German bier-keller... Swords, masks, all sorts of queer carvings dangle from the roof, and on the walls are curious unframed canvases...[23] *With his hands in his coat pockets* [Aristide Bruant] *saunters to and fro, chanting rather than singing, in a loud, monotonous voice to the accompaniment of a piano, played by a one-eyed man... The whole matter is an attempt to do something more realistic than has ever been done before; it succeeds in its painful pity, because Aristide Bruant, both as writer and as singer, is a true artist.*[24]

The difficulty of locating the venue, the possibility of being refused entry, the strange décor and the one-eyed pianist, all evoke a bohemian, distinct world full of ritual and signs, which must be observed by the uninitiated.

Arthur Symons visited Le Chat Noir cabaret in 1892. His description presents a similar vision of underground, illicit, entertainment. Rodolphe Salis, a failed painter, had opened the Chat Noir in 1882. It soon attracted an intellectual crowd, and was renowned for its Chinese-inspired shadow plays. Salis was later to proclaim: 'God created the world, Napoleon founded the Legion of Honour, and I made Montmartre'.[25] Steinlen's bold poster for Le Chat Noir shows the influence of Japanese woodcuts on the development of French poster design, in terms of composition, the use of flat colours, and outlining.[26] The poster's key components – a stark simplicity yet an immediately arresting and recognisable image – became essential ingredients of successful poster design (plate 30).

Interestingly, in his description of Le Chat Noir, Symons sets the scene with direct reference to London's Soho, and clearly guides the reader through the club's protocol to help him plan his visit. His audience is obviously English, and male. The overall atmosphere is one of an exotic, yet safe, cultural experience, where you could observe Montmartre's types.

... you turn into a little, narrow street, a sort of less exclusive Wardour Street, and there, with a curiosity shop on one side of it and a curiosity shop in front, you find a queer, black, whimsical structure bearing the sign of a Black Cat... Symons then helps the reader plan his own visit: *It is not worth going to the Chat Noir at any time but about nine in the evening; if you go then you will find the wooden tables pretty plentifully covered with glasses, and you will have a chance of studying the habitués of the place before the performance upstairs begins. Meanwhile you must take your ticket at the bar, where the large and benign Madame Salis will write it for you. At 9.30 there is a movement in the place; people with rolls of music enter and are gaily hailed by their friends as they pass... You give up your ticket, a mysterious curtain is drawn back, and you proceed to mount a steep ascent of narrow stairs. The staircase winds and turns, you climb wonderingly, meeting at every turn some new freak of decoration, there are placards in wood, painted with the laws of this little realm...*[27] Symons then describes the theatre upstairs and each successive act, including the famous dance of shadows.

Symons' descriptions of the cabarets are evocative in their physical descriptions and guiding hand through this nightime world. The following description reveals his attitude towards the inhabitants of Montmartre, and of his reading of Lautrec's work which he associates with the depravity he sees.[28]

In depraved vision [Lautrec] *leans over the abyss of hell and gazes unperturbed on the agonies of the damned. Perturbed he indicates the insane desires of woman for man, of human reptile for human reptile, the murderous divisions of the sexes... Yet these degraded beings, who endure callously enough their degradation, are not created by a man who hates them; he paints them as they are and not as they are... They stand as he makes them stand – stupid beyond stupidity, beautiful, perverse, inhuman; he sets them in motion when he chooses to, and we see the skirts of the dancing women in the air, and the slower rhythms of their dances. one knows, certainly, where* [these women] *exist: in evil houses, in the streets, in the balls, in the café-concerts, in the music-halls; and that they are always astonishingly alive.*[29]

These descriptions of the women of Montmartre possibly reflects society's fears of the dangers of contracting syphilis, a (then) incurable sexually transmitted disease that could lead to madness and early death. According to Rounding, by the late nineteenth century, as many as twenty per cent of the Paris population was affected.[30]

Symons, however, appreciated talent, and seems to recognise it as a redeeming force.[31] He explores the history of the *chahut* and its dance moves at some length, even

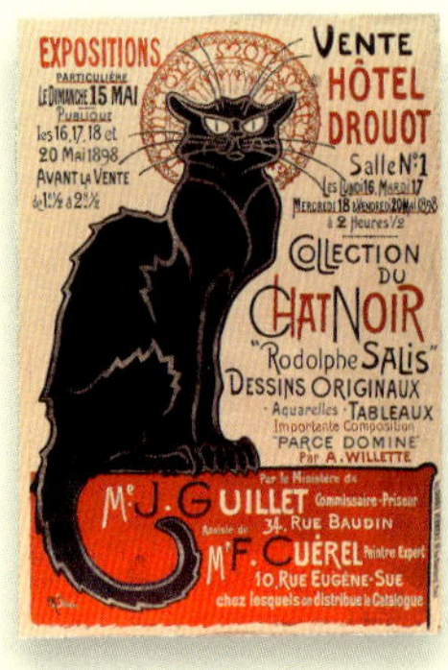

Plate 30
(Above & detail, right)
Théophile-Alexandre Steinlen
(1859–1923)
Collection du Chat Noir
1898
COLOUR LITHOGRAPH
135 x 102 cm
Bridgeman Art Library Bibliotèque des Art Décoratifs, Paris
This poster is the later version than that exhibited in 1894 and shows how artists adapted their original poster design for different products.

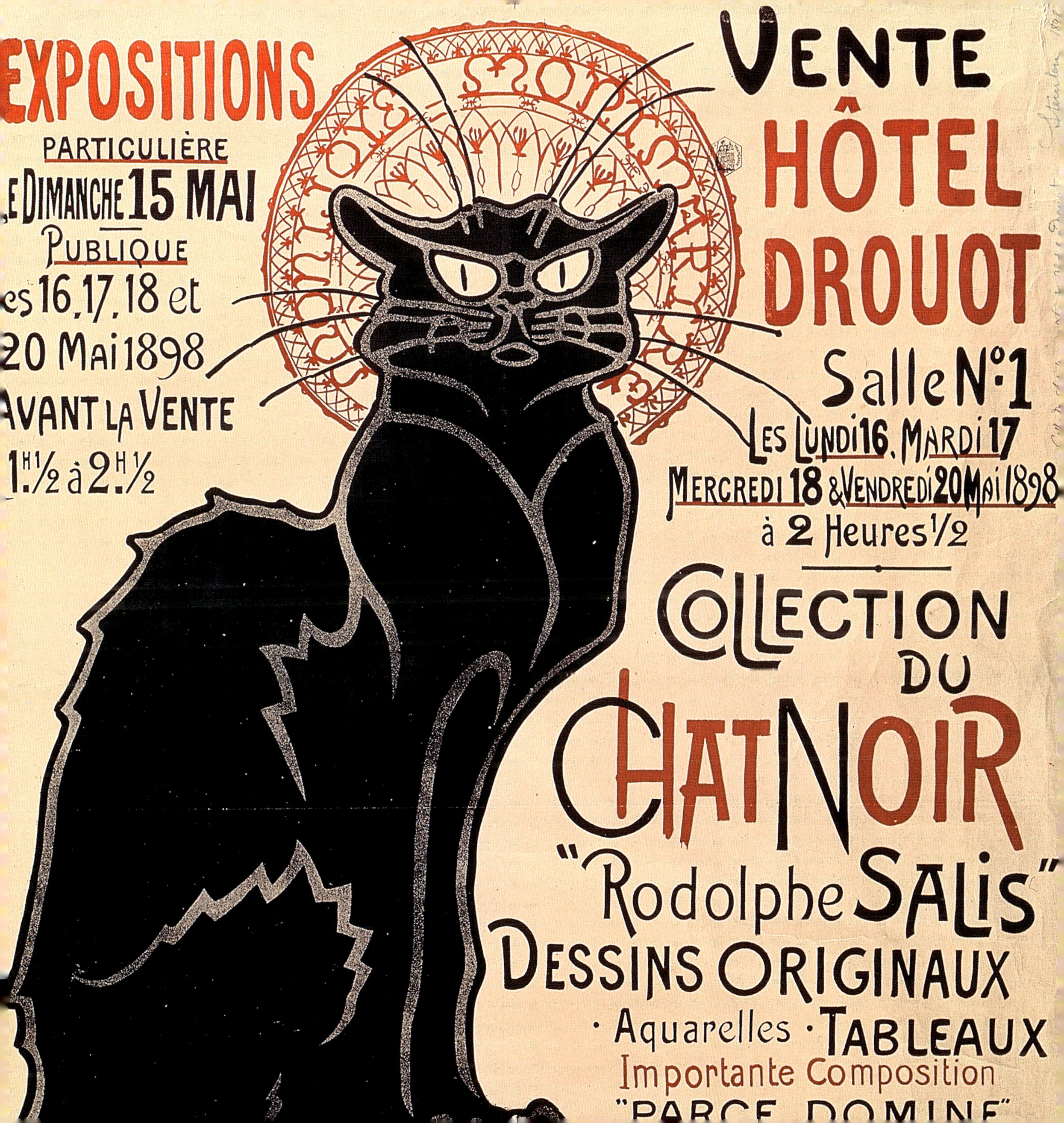
EXPOSITIONS
PARTICULIÈRE
E DIMANCHE 15 MAI
PUBLIQUE
es 16, 17, 18 et
20 Mai 1898
AVANT LA VENTE
1H½ à 2H½
VENTE
HÔTEL
DROUOT
Salle N°1
LES LUNDI 16, MARDI 17
MERCREDI 18 & VENDREDI 20 MAI 1898
à 2 Heures ½
COLLECTION
DU
CHAT NOIR
"Rodolphe SALIS"
DESSINS ORIGINAUX
· Aquarelles · TABLEAUX
Importante Composition
"PARCE DOMINE"

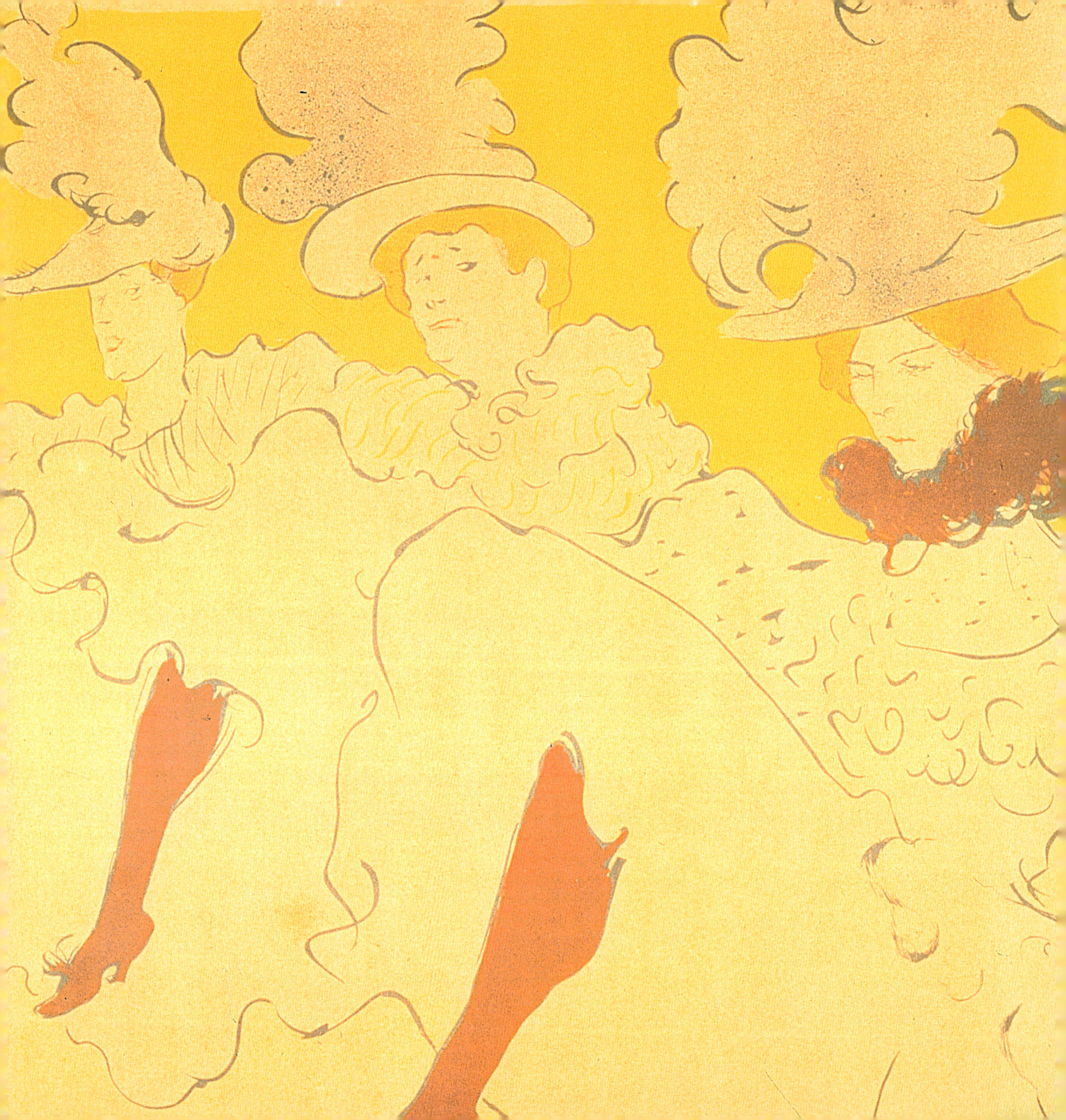

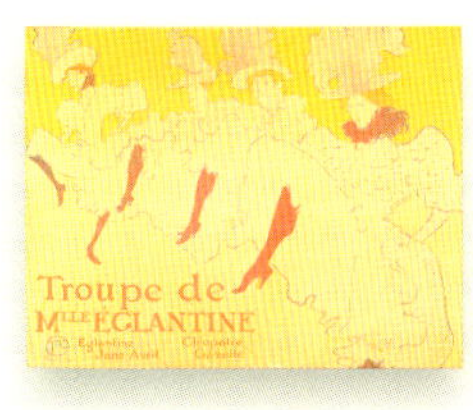

Plate 31
(above & detail, left)
Henri
de Toulouse-Lautrec
(1864–1901)
Troupe de Mlle.
Eglantine
1895–6
COLOUR LITHOGRAPH
63.5 X 81 CM
V&A Images/Victoria
& Albert Museum
An example was
shown at the London
poster exhibition 1896,
No. 125 (3/- or 15p)

attending a dance class by the famous cabaret dancer Nini Pattes-en-l'air (Nini Legs-in-the-air). His description is as follows:

... it was at the Jardin de Paris, about the year 1884, that the chahut, or the quadrille naturaliste, made its appearance, and, with La Goulue and Grille-d'Egout, [The Glutton and The Drain, two famous dancers] *came to stay. The dance is simply a quadrille in delirium – a quadrille in which the steps are punctuated by le port d'armes (or high kicks), with le grand écart (or 'the splits') for parenthesis.* (PLATE 31) *Le port d'armes is done by standing on one foot and holding the other upright in the air; le grand écart by sitting on the floor with the legs absolutely horizontal. Beyond these two fundamental rules of the game, everything almost is left to the fantasy of the performer, and the fantasy of the whirling people of the Moulin-Rouge... Even in Paris you must be somewhat ultra-modern to appreciate it, and to join, night after night, those avid circles which form so rapidly here and there on the ball-room floor, as a waltz-rhythm ends, and a placard bearing the words 'Quadrille' is hung out from the musicians' gallery.*[32]

In contrast to Symons' portrayal of Montmartre as exotic, dark, 'other', the French author Marcel de Bare, similarly writing his memoirs of the Moulin Rouge in the 1920s when there were rumours of its reopening, describes a friendly, intimate environment, mostly peopled by regulars, in which the armchairs are comfortable, the entrance and the drinks affordable, and the entertainment varied'.[33] Rather than present the Moulin Rouge as simply a night time event, with all the connotations that implies, Bare evokes a cabaret that catered for all types and classes, and that attracted different audiences on weekdays and weekends, during the day or at night.

Intriguing as these later written descriptions are, it was the poster that provided the immediate visual images of Parisian nightlife first seen by an English audience in 1894, in the poster exhibition at the Royal Aquarium.

Today, the posters of this period and the publication of memoirs related to it, are now inextricably woven into our understanding of this time and place in French history. The skill of Lautrec and his contemporaries have ensured the enduring recognition of the places and people of *Belle Époque* Paris, and the goods and entertainments advertised through the medium of the poster. The Moulin Rouge, Jane Avril, Aristide Bruant, Montmartre: these names remain in the public's consciousness due to the remarkable skill of these early poster artists, and in particular, the skill of one man, Henri de Toulouse-Lautrec. Lautrec's name is synonymous with the Moulin Rouge, despite its having preoccupied him for only a short period in his life. Yet his creative genius at this moment produced a body of work which continues to determine our perception of Paris of the *Belle Époque*.

Claire Jones

Footnotes

1 Margaret Timmers, *The Power of the Poster*, London, 1998.
2 Philip Dennis Cate and Sinclair Hamilton Hitchings, *The Color Revolution: Color Lithography in France 1890–1900*, Santa Barbara and Salt Lake City, 1978, p. 10.
3 For information on Lautrec, see for example *Toulouse-Lautrec* (exhibition catalogue), New Haven and London, 1991.
4 'The Art of the Poster – A French Master', *The Sketch*, April 1, 1896, p. 426.
5 Henri de Toulouse-Lautrec, *Correspondance*, Gallimard, 1992, no. 386; Edward Gordon Craig, *Index to the Story of My Days*, London, 1957, p. 150; Frank Rutter, *Art in My Time*, London, 1933, pp. 45–6.
6 *London Metropolitan Archives*: LCC Theatres Committee Papers – Royal Aquarium 1888–1903 (LCC/MIN/10, 891).
7 Maurice Rickards, *Banned Posters*, London, 1969, pp. 22–30.
8 A. S. Hartrick, *A Painter's Pilgrimage Through Fifty Years*, Cambridge, 1939, p. 92.
9 The French originally referred to this period as the *fin de siècle*, or the end of the century, but during the course of the twentieth century this period of French history has become mythologised for its decadence and is now more often referred to as the *Belle Époque*.
10 Émile Zola, *Au Bonheur des Dames*, 1883.
11 J. Williamson, *Decoding Advertisements*, 1978, p. 12.
12 See for example M Ryan's *Prostitution in London, with a comparative view of that of Paris and New York*, 1839, and A J B Parent-Duchâtelet, *De la Prostitution dans la ville de Paris*, 1836.
13 *Montmartre and the making of mass culture*, ed. Gabriel P Weisberg, 2001, p. 77. Weisberg refers to V. A. Zelizer's *Pricing the Priceless Child: Changing Social Values of Children*, 1994, which traces the emergence of the modern child, at once economically 'useless' and emotionally 'priceless', from the late 1800s to the 1930s. Zelizer terms this the 'sacralisation' of child life.
14 Chéret produced various posters for Saxoléine in this same format, mainly distinguishable by the colour of the women's dresses.
15 By obscuring the women's bodies behind the wall, Pal possibly avoided the dilemma of having to deal with the rather tricky issue of appropriate cycling attire for women, although by the 1890s, cycling bloomers were worn in France, but not readily accepted in England.
16 Robert Goldman, *Reading Ads Socially*, 1992, p. 23.
17 G P Weisberg, *Montmartre and the Making of Mass Culture*, 2001, p. 149.
18 *Le Moulin Rouge – La Goulue*, was exhibited at Les XX, February 1892, Association pour l'Art Antwerp, May 1892, Independents April to May 1892.
19 Interestingly, Bruant preferred Steinlen to Lautrec, because, according to Sweetman, '*he* [Steinlen] *avoided such disturbing images* [as Lautrec's], *confining himself to the comedy of the streets rather than trying to see beyond into the misery and*

degradation that was the lot of many of those who were so glibly transformed into stock caricatures'. David Sweetman, *Toulouse-Lautrec and the Fin de Siècle,* 1999, p. 153.

20 David Sweetman, *Toulouse-Lautrec and the Fin de Siècle,* 1999, p. 156. Montmartre has a history of political activism which is most evident in its role in the Paris Commune of 1871, when its women ran down the hill to burn the Tuileries Palace, and the notorious nightclubs and dance halls were transformed into workplaces which supported the Commune and its socialist and anarchist ideologies. Despite the fall of the Commune and the installation of the Third Republic, some artists and venues continued to provide entertainment with a distinctly political edge. One such venue was the Taverne de Bagne, named after a slang word for prison, where the waiters wore prison garb accessorised with a ball and chain.

21 Arthur Symons, *Parisian Nights, a book of essays,* 1926, and *From Toulouse-Lautrec to Rodin, with some personal impressions,* 1929.

22 Arthur Symons, *Parisian Nights, a book of essays,* 1926, p.20.

23 This possibly refers to works by Lautrec, who produced seven paintings directly related to Bruant's songs, including *À St Lazarre, À la Grenelle, À la Bastille,* and *À Montrouge.* At one time at least ten works by Lautrec hung at Bruant's cabaret.

24 Arthur Symons, *Parisian Nights, a book of essays,* 1926, pp. 11–13.

25 Salis would sell *Le Chat Noir* to Aristide Bruant in 1885.

26 The term *Japonisme* was first coined in 1872 by Philippe Burty, a French art critic, to describe the influence of Japanese style on French art. Japanese objects had flowed into the West from the 1850s onwards, and attracted the attention of both artists and collectors. The Paris Exposition Universelle of 1867 brought Japanese arts to the attention of a wider public.

27 Arthur Symons, *Parisian Nights, a book of essays,* 1926, pp. 21–24.

28 Despite associating Lautrec with the depravity he saw in Montmatre, Symons had a great respect for the artist.

29 Arthur Symons, *From Toulouse-Lautrec to Rodin, with some personal impressions,* 1929, pp. 4–5.

30 Virginia Rounding, *Grandes Horizontales, The Lives and Legends of Four Nineteenth Century Courtesans,* Bloomsbury, 2003.

31 Indeed, Symons owned at least one poster by Lautrec, of Jane Avril from 1899.

32 Arthur Symons, *From Toulouse-Lautrec to Rodin, with some personal impressions,* 1929, pp. 24–25. Symons continues to describe the *guitare,* and other *chahut* moves.

33 Marcel de Bare, *Les Meniers du Moulin Rouge, anécdotes et souvenirsínedits sur le Bal célébre,* 1925, p. 355.

Appendix *Contemporary reviews and advertisements of the poster exhibitions of 1894–5 and 1896*

***Morning Advertiser*, 24 October 1894, front page**

TODAY – ROYAL AQUARIUM – The most EXTRAORDINARY EXHIBITION of the CENTURY – An EXHIBITION of ARTISTIC PICTORIAL POSTERS by the greatest living French and English Artists. No extra charge. All entertainments as usual. Early performances 11.15 am. The Annamites, Theatre 4 and 9. Great Central Stage Performance, 2. 30 and 7. 30. A Marvellous Show. Ballad Concert, 5. 50. Swimming, 5 and 10. Skating, three sessions etc. Through tickets, with admission, by District Rail. Notice – Herr Berg's 30 hour's Remarkable Pianoforte Recital will commence at 4 pm on Friday

***Pall Mall Gazette*, 23 October 1894, and subsequent days had this front page advertisement, THE ROYAL AQUARIUM**

At No Place in the World Can so many sights be seen as the Royal Aquarium

Artistic Poster Exhibition. The Annamites, 4 and 8. Conjuring (free) 11am. La Fluer's Circus, &c, 12 noon. Fear Training 1.45. Cross 1.55. Grand Varieties, 2.30 and 7.30. All Free. A Marvellous and Extraordinary Show. Woman *v.* Man. The Flying Fitzroys. Fuller's Great Dive. The Great Merritt. A Convict's Escape. Baume and Annie Luker's Great Dives. The Boxing Kangaroo. Rivalli in a Cage of Fire. Adelina Ontario, the graceful Gymnast. Zarmo, upside-down juggler. Alvanti, Wire Funambulist. Zuliana, the Female Samson, *&c.* Ballad Concert 5.50. All Free, Swimmng 5 and 10. Richards v. Brereton, 3 and 8. Skating, &c. 3 Sessions

***Black and White*, 10 November 1894, pp. 602–603, MURAL DECORATIVE ART**

New conditions of life and society evolve new forms of art. The art which would live, to use a felicitous term of current playhouse slang, must be up-to-date. Plantagenet England has its great window stainers; medieval Venice her fresco painters and mosaic workers; modern Paris her poster designers. We have long heard of Willette, Grasset, Sinet, Forain, Steinlen, Chéret and the rest, and those of us who travel have seen their work in the windows of the boulevard kiosks and on the walls of Paris; but nothing has been attempted to bring home to us here in England what was really being done, and why the Paris poster was so immeasurably superior to the English placard. We can now no longer complain on that score. Two hundred of the best examples of the French designers bedeck the balconies of the Westminster Aquarium, and with them is shown the newest English work.

It seems strange that London, the richest and, in matters of commercial advertising, the most speculative city in Europe, should so lag behind Paris in this question of street bills. The truth is, it was not want of funds or enterprise that kept us back – it was our gross stupidity and ineptitude to understand the demands of the new conditions. Our great advertisers were willing to give incredible sums for wall advertisement designs. It was useless to appeal to our more famous painters direct. They were much too high and mighty to draw for the bill-sticker; so the big manufacturers bought popular and humorous works, already painted, from Burlington House itself, from eminent R.A.s in fact. These they reproduced at enormous cost, and surrounding them with mock gold frames in printed paper, they plastered them over every blank wall. The effect was hideous; and the distorted pictures were unspeakably out of place, and shamefully disfigured the sites they appeared. Now and then an artist half seized the real idea. This you can see at the Aquarium today. Poor Fred Walker knew what he wanted when he designed the fine black-and-white figure going out of an open door into the night for Wilkie Collins' novel *The Woman in White*, but he wasted his strength in elaborate draperies. Professor Herkomer came nearer the need when he produced the sterling figure that was used when this paper was first issued – that, at least, had power and simplicity. But though the Dudley Hardys, the Greiffenhagens, Raven Hills, and Phil Mays of to-day may be only imitators of Chéret, Lautrec and company at present, they are distinctly beginning to understand the new laws of the new art, and ultimately must develop a native school. They have no false pride; they work direct for the hoardings. There is already much. So far two or three excellent posters have been produced. Mr. Dudley Hardy, whom the dislike of London to the nude handicaps with practical drapery in his work, has given us in *'To-Day'* a work of elemental simplicity and strength which meets the first essential of a poster – it arrests attention. But alive and vigorous as it is, it is only a figure on a bill; it does not decorate the space it fills well. Very much better is his *'St. Paul's'*, the dignified and effective young lady in olive with a lily in her hand. She furnished the complete decoration of the whole oblong she is drawn to adorn. Mr. Maurice Greiffenhagen's powerful announcement of the new series of a contemporary [magazine?] is on the right lines: well disposed masses of ungraduated colour, and very simple in line; but it is not quite enough like a woman to be strong in human interest.

Now turn to the Frenchmen. A good poster must, before all things, arrest the attention of the passer by; it must decorate, and it must interest; its composition must be exceedingly simple in colour, mass, line, and light, and shade. See how the genius of Jules Chéret grasps and combines these necessary qualities. No question of him despising the public walls; he designs for them direct, and on the stone itself, since he, like several of his colleagues, is a skilled practical lithographer and knows exactly what are the extreme potentialities of his material, and how speedily to reach them. Most of his subjects are dancing girls partly clad in scarlets, yellows and blues so gauzy that they betray the somewhat angular limbs they would cover, and enhance the corybantic fury of their motion. They are full of 'go', and not ungraceful; and the very spirits of the wicked Paris of our dreams. Though so glaring the colours harmonize. The five Saxoléine posters advertise a lamp oil, and women with bare shoulders variously tending lamps beneath their wide-spreading silk shades afford splendid opportunities for effective arrangement of transparent colour and strongly contrasted chiaroscuro. Chéret has designed four hundred posters. Forty of them are here. M. E. Grasset is entirely medieval in feeling. He is an ecclesiastic window stainer born out of time. His *'Joanne d'Arc'* poster for Mdme. Bernhardt has a fine romantic sentiment, and his poster for the Romantic Library is a Sir Thomas Lawrence sort of lady in black with a large lace collar, reading by a lamp in an elaborate picture. Note the touch of character in the loose white stocking and slatternly ankle, a mark of the absorbed reader. But such work would be rather wasted at a distance. And here we may remark that this example is in great request with collectors, and that as much as ten francs must be given for a copy of it, for poster-collecting is the latest hobby. M. Steinlen is one of the most artistic of the poster-men. His tall posters of Yvette Guilbert singing over the Café Chantant footlights are marvels in their way. M. Lautrec I take to be the greatest artist of them all. He affects quieter colours than his fellows: black, olive, brown, scarlet, lemon and orange. His effects are obtained with a minimum of labour, masses of ungraduated colour, and the fewest possible strong lines. His faces are full of character, and when he desires, are terribly grim or comic. Probably the best poster, taking all the requirements into consideration, shown is his *'Bruant at his Inn'*, the head and shoulders of a sardonic-visaged man in profile, who wears a huge slouch hat, which is one piece of black, an Inverness cape, which is another, and a red wrapper round the throat, the end of which is tossed back over the shoulders. Seen across the width of the Aquarium this dominates everything shown; and the powerful face grips the spectator more as he draws nearer and studies it. Close by is his poster of 'Le Matin', a criminal brought bound to the scaffold, his face tinted pale green, the most terribly dramatic piece of symbolic colour you can conceive; and behind, on the white ground, are tall, helmeted, cloaked and mounted soldiers in black silhouette. No need to ask the man in the street to stop and look at this. M. Boutet de Monvel, who brings the most delicate poetry to play on his work, is surely too dainty for the street; but Sinet, Ibels, Willette, Métivet, and others send notable work, on which only space prevents my enlarging. The general effect of this poster gallery is not dissimilar to that of the group of impressions one sees at the N. E. A. C.; but what is often preposterous in the young Englishman's cabinet picture is merely pregnant caricature very much in place in the poster; and to what a splendid poster M. Bésnard's 'Orange and Blue', at the New Gallery, might be adapted! R. J. -S.

Court Journal, October, 1894

The French artists produce some beautiful work; light, bright, and intelligent. The colours are harmonious yet striking as they should be, for the purpose of attracting the eye. Parisians are not content with mere blocks of men and women with mechanically executed features, they aspire to invest their figures with movement and facial expression, the result is that wall pictures are produced which are a pleasure to the public, and must be a profit to the advertiser.

Pall Mall Gazette, quoted in *The Billposter*, 1 December 1894

The exhibits are 'intended to appeal from a distance amidst the sights and colours of real life in the streets, they rely scarcely at all on detail, and for the most part gain little by close inspection. In the Aquarium, then, with noise, crowds, and no lack of other excitements, posters are seen, as they should be, asserting themselves in a place that has more kinship with the streets than with the ordinary picture gallery... but the man whose path of duty leads him to the Aquarium at this moment [is an?] advertiser, who may learn there how to push his wares, conciliate a public whom he had justly incensed, and also contribute to a picture show for many whose only gallery is the street.... posters must advertise as well as please, while to do either they must attract without the aid of a frame an attention that is beckoned on all sides, as a traveller by hotel touts. Therefore, make them bold, simple and space-penetrating. Let them have something of the virtue of a lighthouse or fog signal. Again, they must be printed in quantities; therefore avoid subtleties which will not reproduce. This exhibition serves to show how much can be done with one or two flat tints broadly disposed; with a mere patch of black against white if it detaches in a piquant silhouette; with a few lines sufficiently bold, summary and eloquent in expression, with an aspect of mystery that tempts elucidation, though this last verges on dangerous ground. Above all, it appears that the poster should not attempt, as so many of our theatrical advertisements do, any emulation of the subject picture. For even when not executed by inadequate artists it is at least always rendered in such an inadequate and unsuitable medium. Such posters look vulgar, and cheap, instead of effective, not because they are large and simplified, but because they pretend to qualities and subtleties foreign to their nature. A good poster is not a bad imitation of something else, but a separate work of art in which lines, tints or whatever may be used are in themselves interesting, as well as effectively combined... Lettering is a difficulty not yet altogether overcome in the development of the poster. It should be clear and large, should form part of the design, and should never seem stamped on as a commercial afterthought.

Westminster Gazette, 22 October 1894, ARTISTIC POSTERS AT THE AQUARIUM

Quite one of the most interesting shows which have been offered to Londoners for some time is the Exhibition of Artistic Posters now open at the Aquarium. They order these things better in France than we do in England, we all know; and here the uninitiated are afforded a most excellent opportunity of seeing how they do it. The whole of the gallery is given up to the purposes of the show, and a remarkably complete collection, embodying examples of nearly all the most famous exponents of this branch of art on both sides of the Channel, has been got together. The exigencies of space have necessitated the restriction of the present show mainly to the works of French and English artists; specimens of the products, of other countries in this direction are promised on a future occasion. There is no gainsaying the interest of the show. It is an astonishing collection. Reform? It is a revolution which is being brought about. Who began it? – it is not easy to say. Certainly Chéret was among the earliest to realise the artistic possibilities of the hoarding, and here you may see some fifty of his finest efforts, including the whole of the famous Buttes Chumont [sic] series, the various Saxoléine designs (among the most remarkable in the whole gallery for combined power and refinement), the Folies-Bergère pictures of Loïe Fuller (in four schemes of colour) and many more as familiar to the Parisian as the Louvre or the Madeleine. Lautrec, too – how shall one describe his amazing creations? If Chéret seduces, Lautrec knocks you down. And from the standpoint of the poster either method will serve. Perhaps there is nothing more vigorous than his Caudieux, nothing more brutally unpleasant that his *'Reine de Joie'*, in the whole series. And praise more acceptable to M. Lautrec than this one may presume it would be difficult to find. Of another stamp is the work of Grasset – less original, less powerful, more solid, yet artistic. Very attractive also are the designs of Bonnard (and additionally interesting from the fact, which may not be generally known, that to Bonnard's example Lautrec traces his own introduction to the hoarding) of Steinlen, of Ibels, of Métivet, of Willette, and others too numerous to particularise. Nor must one for one instant overlook the many admirable examples of our native artists, which find place upon the walls. If few as yet, they are at any rate fit, and whether as regards brilliancy of colour or effectiveness of design, some of the efforts of Dudley Hardy, of Herkomer, of Crane, Steer, Greiffenhagen, Aubrey Beardsley, and the rest, will compare meritoriously with the very best that their Gallic rivals have given us. Of course, the famous Avenue Theatre poster by the last-named is not omitted, while close by in amusing juxtaposition, is the no less famous Oxford skit by 'Weirdsly Dawbery'. Mention should also be made of the brilliantly-successful designs contributed by Messrs. Pride [sic] and Nicholson, who are pleased to be known to the public as the Brothers Beggarstaff, while hard by one should not overlook Fred Walker's admirable *'Woman in White'* design, which is there to remind the thoughtless that the artistic poster is not such a thing of yesterday in this country as some would have us believe. Millais' *'Bubbles'*, by the way, is rather mercifully omitted. Sambourne's cigarette-smoking young lady, on the other hand, might well have been included. But, in general the collection seems commendably complete and the Honorary Committee, who, with Messrs. Edward Bella and G. de Malherbe as executive, have been responsible for the work, may be congratulated upon the results of their labours. Is it too much to hope, by way of conclusion, that the Aquarium authorities, whose posters of all others are the most frankly 'British', will not be ranked among those who fail to profit henceforward from the exhibition now within their walls?

Yorkshire Weekly Post, 11 November 1894, p. 5, SOME ARTISTIC BILLPOSTERS

Early in the eighties Professor Herkomer, enthusiastic as he always is, tilted a lance at the everyday advertisement on the hoardings, and pointed out the admirable opportunities lost for an artistic education, we may almost say, of the eye, which would be bound to impress itself so that even the most cursory observer might profit. The vision was a bright one! We were to have on each posting station a gallery of bills executed by the most brilliant artists of the day, commissioned by the most lavish advertiser we know so well. Each railway station, instead of being an inferno, would be a thing of beauty – if not a joy forever – through passenger trains would be at a discount, for every traveller would be anxious to stay at each roadside station in order to study its gallery – advertisers of cough cures would reap a double benefit from the colds caught by lingering over a very choice 'bit' and soaps would be at a premium to wash away the stain of journeys made longer by the passenger's enthusiasm.

As a pledge of his sincerity the Professor designed an expansive poster in hue for the *'Magazine of Art'*, which depicted the great painters of all ages and nations met together; and his students at Bushey carried out some few commissions on the same idea, notably a most charming block line for one of the Exhibitions; but somehow these admirable efforts fell flat. It seemed that one, and the principal reason for their non-success was the fact that they were not striking enough – there was not sufficient to strike the passerby and arrest his casual eye – though all who stopped to observe were bound to admire. The taste also for black and white work was then uncultivated, and therefore the appreciation relied to a great extent on the artistic temperament of the observer, and, as we venture to think, the artistic temperament is in a minority, the effect was therefore limited. Later, a well-known soap firm, at the end of a very large expenditure for their then current year, produced the famous *'Bubbles'*, a most beautiful and costly reproduction from Millais. Another soap firm replied with some charming monochrome drawings, to which however, as much as ever, the previous drawbacks applied. In the French esprit and brilliant sense of effect and colour, however, was to be found the remedy, and during the last few years Paris has founded a school of artists who have devoted themselves to the artistic designing of *'l'affiche illustré'*. Their high priest has been one Chéret, whose previous experience as a lithographer was a most suitable training for the work he had taken in hand. The example here given of his work is peculiarly characteristic of his pencil and brush. It has the distinct French sentiment of a *'fin-de-siècle'* Watteau. For our columns the drawing has been reduced into line, which, we are afraid, robs it of some force of expression; whilst the delicate but brilliant colour is impossible to express here until the colour printer has worked his promised miracle. At the same time we venture to think that it may convey some idea of the effect. It is a bill for M. Ed. Sagot, a French bookseller, who, prompted by the enthusiastic collectors who have been springing up with the posters themselves, has actually published an illustrated catalogue of the bills he has collected, and for which he finds a ready sale to the amateur. The catalogue itself, illustrated in colours, is a charming specimen of French lithography. Perhaps Chéret's most successful rival, or rather companion, has been Grasset, an example of whom we give. It will be noticed that there is a medieval conventionalism which is peculiarly expressive of the artist's training as a designer of stained glass, but which, to our mind, distinctly adds to the character and effect of the work. The bill itself is an advertisement for an ink, and has now decorated almost every hoarding in France for the last year. Grasset has however, shown more particularly in his Libraire Romantique, of charming and surprising grace, whilst in the opinion of the collector his *'Fête de Paris'* is a classic.

One of the most charming drawings, however, has been produced by almost the newest recruit to the school. Steinlen's work, powerful and expressive at it is in chalks and black and white, has for some time made the front page of *'Gil Blas'* an attraction, but, unfortunately, has been confined to depicting the victims of debauchery and misery in a style distinctly unsuited to the 'young person'. By a strange anomaly, however, the master of the expression of absinthe has achieved a remarkable success in an advertisement for milk! The simplicity and grace of the drawing is perfect, and shows that the genius of the artist can adapt itself with facility to its subject. His drawing of the purring, friendly cats, too, is masterly, and in direct contrast to those of the feline companions of the witches and walkyries of a recent number of *'Gil Blas'*.

All tourists on the Continent during the present year must have been struck by the particularly beautiful drawings issued by the various railway companies – a view, a characteristic figure, and a bunch of flowers give a most rosy idea of the different resorts depicted. In England, the peculiarly adaptive talent of Dudley Hardy has given us the Yellow Girl – a most successful début, and one which must have impressed itself upon our readers, but which has not been intensified by his *'St. Paul's'* which followed. Aubrey Beardsley also designed a poster for the Avenue Theatre some months back, which, however, was only an enlarged drawing similar to those published in the Yellow Book, and which showed that whatever form Mr. Oscar Wilde's protégé's genius may take, his forte is distinctly not colour. By far, however, the most successful English production is that by Mr. Maurice Griffenhagen [sic], who can express colour most clearly in his ordinary black and white drawings. He therefore started with a distinct advantage, which showed itself in the well-known *'Pall Mall'* poster.

This article has been prompted by the exhibition of posters now being held at the Westminster Aquarium, and which is being most successfully patronized, not the least interesting item to its visitors being the tasteful catalogue. All the bills we have mentioned and some 200 others are upon its walls, although for the examples given here the writer has drawn upon the collection of Mr. Arthur L. Knight of Basinghall Street – a most enthusiastic amateur. We are bound to believe that although the most successful instances up to the present have been by Frenchmen, or following their manner, still their success will prompt the English school to assert itself, and that in addition to the R. A. of the black and white draughtsmen prophesied by Mr. Harry Furniss, we may have a P. R. A. of the hoardings. W. J. Warren

The Sketch, 1 April 1896, p. 426, THE EXHIBITION AT THE AQUARIUM

The Poster Exhibition now being held at the Royal Aquarium equals, and, indeed, surpasses the first one, which took place eighteen months ago. It is worthy of note that its predecessor produced results and modifications now clearly apparent, for the posters of 1895 are a great advance on those produced in previous years. Poster-collectors – for the craze is spreading rapidly – will find much to covet here.

Of the excellent and varied collection of French *'affiches'* shown there is little new to say. Chéret remains indisputably first, and his work has the further advantage of thoroughly fulfilling the business requirements of those whose goods he has been commissioned to advertise. He is equally happy when calling attention to a poetic pantomine (*'L'Enfant Prodigue'*) or setting forth the merits of a mineral oil (Saxoléine). Still, as he deals almost entirely with red, yellow and blue, rather than with secondary or composite tints, there is a certain sameness about his work, and it is, of course, plain that his *'affiches'* are literally designed for the hoarding, and not intended for close or detailed examination. Lautrec, if he is to be judged from the six examples exhibited, indulges in entirely different methods. With the exception of the *'Eglantine Troupe'*, where he gives an idealised and graceful group of the dancers in question, he pays little or no attention to the class of subject advertised. His effort is rather to produce a successful design, a striking picture, than to tell a story or illustrate a fact; and his success as a poster-painter probably depends on the fact that he, on the whole, appeals to an artistic public quick to appreciate and notice good work.

Grasset and Steinlen are both represented, the former by an advertisement of the June number of the *'Century'*, which compares curiously with the work of Bradley, Rhead and Penfield. Indeed, all the American exhibits are strikingly individual, and their designers seem to have borrowed little or nothing from the French or English branches of the art. Entirely eschewing the immense posters which are now so universal in London and Paris, the American artists content themselves with designs rarely occupying more than nineteen by fourteen inches – indeed, E. Penfield's *'Harper'* posters are, in a sense, as highly finished as are many easel-pictures; and, in several of his most successful designs, that for May 1894, and those for June, August and October of 1895, he utilises a considerable knowledge of landscape art with excellent effect. Bradley's *'Chapbook'* designs are also exceptionally charming, and explain the present American poster-collecting mania.

Mr. Dudley Hardy, who is adequately represented, possesses all the qualities which distinguish Jules Chéret's work, and yet each of his designs is strongly individual, and he is far more daring as regards colouring than the French artist ever cares to be. He also greatly differs from Chéret in the composition of his large posters, for the latter rarely makes use of one figure, while Mr. Hardy, especially in his later work, has not feared to group together three, four, and five figures. He was also, apparently, the first to use the picturesque bicycle in a pictorial sense, and his *'Cycling at Olympia'* is instinct with life and movement.

Mr. Edward Bella has been fortunate in obtaining so many characteristic specimens of the 'Brothers Beggarstaff' posters – several more than those mentioned in the excellent illustrated catalogue. They include the non-published *'Don Quixote'*, as fine a piece of imaginative work as was ever designed for a hoarding. The two artists (Messrs. J. Pryde and W. Nicholson) do not seem to have been really influenced by their Parisian art-training; their work is wholly individual, and up to the present time they have generally contented themselves with the use of a few neutral tints – grey and brown put, of course, in juxtaposition to white or black. Thus, their most successful designs have been stencilled on brown paper, proving once more, if it were necessary to do so, the limitless resources of the silhouette.

Aubrey Beardley's signature is not attached to a single exhibit, but the influence of his strange, uncanny genius is evident in several successful posters. Detaille, Caran d'Ache and his rival Forain, Puvis de Chavannes, and last, not least, Herkomer, are among those exhibitors whose names are not connected with this branch of art.

Sources of contemporary reviews and advertisements of the London poster exhibitions of 1894 and 1896 at the Royal Aquarium

1894 Exhibition

Art in Advertising, 28 October 1894
Athenaeum, 27 October 1894, p. 576
The Billposter, 1 November 1894, p. 1
Black and White, 10 November 1894, pp. 602–603
Court Journal, October 1894
The Daily Chronicle, Wednesday, 24 October 1894, p. 7
The Daily Graphic, 22 Monday October 1894, p. 6
The Daily News, 24 October 1894, p. 6
The Daily Telegraph, 24 October, 1894, p. 4
Fame – a journal for advertisers, 15 November, 1894, pp. 10–11
The Graphic, 3 November 1894, p. 519
The Illustrated London News, supplement, 10 November 1894, p. 2
Leeds Mercury, Monday 5 November 1894, p. 4
The Magazine of Art, January 1895, p. 117
Morning Advertiser, 24 October 1894, front page and p. 5
The Morning Post, 24 October 1894, p. 2, Artistic Advertisements
Newcastle Daily Leader, Thursday 25 October 1894, p. 5
Pall Mall Budget, 25 October 1894, p. 21
Pall Mall Gazette, 23 October 1894, and subsequent days, front page advertisement for THE ROYAL AQUARIUM
Pall Mall Gazette, quoted in *The Billposter*, 1 December 1894
The Penny Illustrated Paper, 10 November 1894, p. 291
Pick-Me-Up, 10 November 1894, 'The Possibilities of the Poster' by L. Raven-Hill
The Queen, 3 November 1894, p. 766, 'The Poster Exhibition' by Clarence Rook
Saturday Review, 15 December 1894, p. 657-8
The Sketch, 7 November 1894, p. 82
The Star, 24 October 1894, p. 3
The Sun, Thursday, 25 October 1894, p. 1
The Times, front page, Tuesday 23 October 1894
The Times, Friday, 26 October 1894
The Times, quoted in *The Billposter*, 1 December 1894
Weekly Dispatch, 21 October 1894
Westminster Gazette, 22 October 1894
The Windsor Magazine, January 1895, by Gleeson White, editor of *The Studio*, quoted in Colin Campbell, *The Beggarstaff Brothers*, London, 1990, p. 33
Woman, 31 October 1894 (by P. E. R.) p. 6
Yorkshire Weekly Post, 11 November 1894, p. 5, 'Some Artistic Billposters' by W. J. Warren.

1896 Exhibition

The Daily Chronicle, Saturday, 21 March 1896
The Daily Graphic, 21 March 1896, p. 14 (or p. 1134)
The Daily News, 21 March 1896, p. 3
Morning Advertiser, 26 March 1896
Morning Advertiser, 3 April 1896
The Sketch, 1 April 1896, p. 426
The Star, 24 March 1896, p. 1
The Times, 26 March 1896, p. 3
Westminster Gazette, 23 March 1896, p. 4

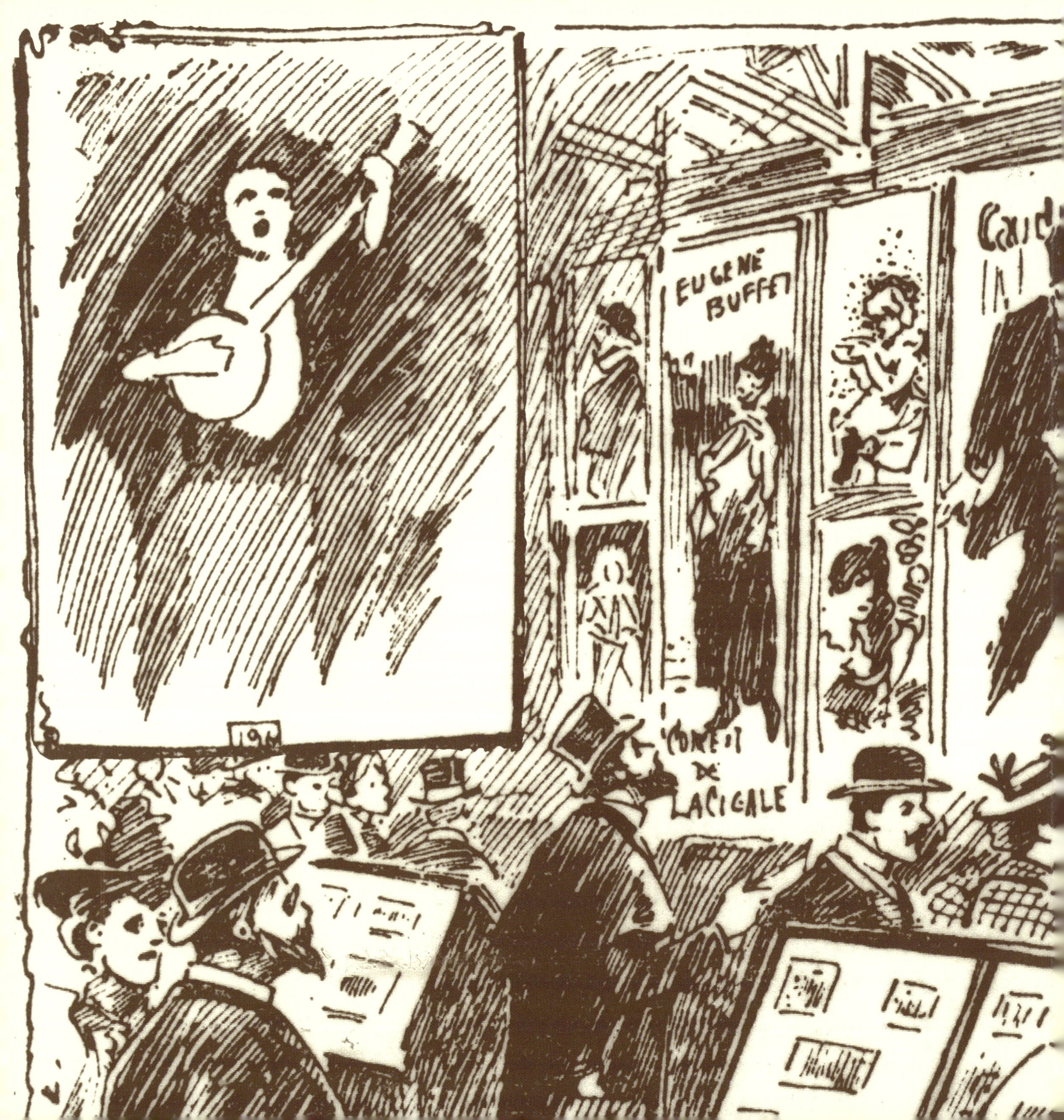
EUGENE BUFFET
DE
LACIGALE